STEV

Foreword by
Eric Brown

It's a privilege to write this foreword for the latest edition of Alan's insightful and irreplaceable personal hotel guide. For many years Alan has pointed travellers in the direction of some of the most beautiful luxury lodgings and exquisite eating places around the country. Skilfully imparting his knowledge, revealing thoughtful details about each one and helping the discerning to find their perfect place to stay or dine.

When recommending hotels and restaurants, Alan has matched them to his own exceptional standards, seeking out places with great service, refined quality and genuine character. The establishments are a treasure of individuality and style, with owners, managers and staff going all out to welcome and care for visitors to their own beautiful part of Scotland.

My life in catering began more than forty years ago, nurtured in a family business of small hotel and luxury country houses, learning to deliver quality service and first class customer care. Hospitality has been transformed over this time with welcomed modern advances in facilities, food, themes and styles, giving customers more choice and much improved luxury. Still, at the heart of this industry is great customer service, a warm genuine welcome and attention to detail. These I believe continue to be the defining attributes of great hospitality.

In Stevenson's guide you will find wonderful places to visit and great people who'll genuinely care for you.

Eric Brown
Roman Camp Country House
Callander, Stirlingshire

1 STEVENSONS 2017

STEVENSONS
SCOTLAND'S
GOOD HOTEL AND FOOD BOOK
2017

Published by:
Alan Stevenson Publications
Fala
20 West Cairn Crescent
Penicuik
Midlothian
EH26 0AR
Tel: 01968 678015
Mobile: 07786 966341
Email: alan@stevensons-scotland.com
www.stevensons-scotland.com

North American Representative:
Ann Litt,
Undiscovered Britain
11978 Audubon Place
Philadelphia, PA 19116
Tel: (215) 969-0542
Fax: (215) 969-9251
Email: annlitt413@gmail.com
www:UndiscoveredBritain.com

Copyright © 2016 Stevensons - Scotland's Good Hotel and Food Book - Twenty-second Edition

ISBN 978-0-9933350-1-3

Price: £10.00
$18.00 from USA agent only. (Includes Canada)
See page 94 for price list plus postage & packaging

Typesetting/Graphics: Colin Shepherd.
Printed in Scotland: J. Thomson Colour Printers, Glasgow.
Front Cover: The MacLeod House, Trump International, Balmedie, Aberdeenshire.

Alan Stevenson
Publisher

*A very warm welcome to STEVENSONS 2017 - the **22nd** edition of Scotland's Good Hotel & Food Book.*

Feedback has been extremely positive and hotels & restaurants have experienced another good year. Although there has been an improvement, Aberdeenshire still 'lags' behind due to the demise of the oil industry. After 'Brexit' the pound fell quite a bit hence an advantage to our visitors from abroad. Also, bookings from the domestic market were encouraging.

My personal selection once again includes properties that maintain the highest standards of hotelkeeping and restaurants that provide a gastronomic delight. Over the past 30 years I have visited and stayed in all parts of Scotland – and am very fortunate to savour what I can only describe as one of the most scenic countries in the world for which I never tire (despite the weather sometimes!).

*Grateful to **Eric Brown** at **Roman Camp Country House** for the Main Foreword and **Craig Wilson** of **'Eat on the Green'** for the Food Foreword. Their contribution to the industry over the years has been immense.*

*Once again I look forward with anticipation to my travels next year when I will compile the **23rd edition** of the book for year 2018. (Also see website: www.stevensons-scotland.com)*

INTRODUCTION

Photo by Yerbury of Edinburgh

STEVENSONS

SCOTLAND'S
GOOD HOTEL AND FOOD BOOK
2017

CONTENTS	PAGE

We do not use growth hormones in any shape or form.

The Scotch Beef Club is unashamedly based on quality.

We offer independent assurance, supported by the Scottish SPCA.

Our members believe strongly in animal welfare.

Our standards are much higher than legislation demands.

Fresh meat is low in salt and high in iron.

Our members are passionate about red meat.

Less stressed animals provide better tasting meat.

We are supported by some of the UK's finest chefs.

Cattle are reared mainly outdoors and fed on a grass diet.

All our livestock are born and raised for all of their lives on assured farms in Scotland.

Modern breeding and butchery standards produce leaner meat.

Looking for a reason to try a Scotch Beef club restaurant?
Well, here's twelve.

Our member restaurants are a cut above the rest. That's why they choose the finest Scotch Beef. With full traceability and guaranteed levels of assurance, Scotch Beef is high on quality, high on taste. So if you care about your food, look for the Scotch Beef Club logo on your next meal out. We can think of at least a dozen reasons why.

 Look out for the member restaurants throughout this guide wherever you see this symbol.

SCOTCH BEEF

THE SCOTCH BEEF CLUB

To find a member restaurant near you, visit: **www.scotchbeefclub.org**

STEVENSONS

SCOTLAND'S
GOOD HOTEL AND FOOD BOOK
2017

AWARDS/SYMBOLS

VisitScotland (Scottish Tourist Board)

The Star System is a world-first. It denotes quality assurance on a range of 1 to 5 stars. This is why it is only the quality of the welcome and service, the food, the hospitality, ambience and the comfort and condition of the property which earns VisitScotland stars, not the size of the accommodation or the range of facilities. Gold stars recognise businesses which constantly achieve the hightest level of excellence within their VisitScotland star rating. This business has excelled in the areas of customer care and hospitality and displays evidence of a real commitment to staff development and training.

The quality grades awarded are, eg:

GOLD

★★★★★	Exceptional, world-class
★★★★	Excellent
★★★	Very Good
★★	Good

AA Red Rosettes

Hotels and restaurants may be awarded red rosettes to denote the quality of food they serve. It is an award scheme, not a classification scheme. They award rosettes annually on a rising scale of one to five.

AA Red Stars ★★★★★

The AA top hotels in Britain and Ireland are assessed and announced annually with a red star award. They recognise the very best hotels in the country that offer consistently outstanding levels of quality, comfort, cleanliness and comfort care. Red stars are awarded on a rising scale of one to five. Restaurants with rooms also qualify for this award.

Bull Logo

Any establishment which displays the Bull Logo is a member of the Scotch Beef Club. The criteria is strict - the product is derived from cattle born, reared for all of their lives, slaughtered and dressed in Scotland. The animals will have been produced in accordance with assurance schemes accredited to European Standard and meeting the standards and assessments set by Quality Meat Scotland's Assurance Schemes.

PLEASE NOTE: THESE AWARDS DO NOT NECESSARILY FORM PART OF MY OVERALL PERSONAL SELECTION OF GOOD HOTELS AND RESTAURANTS IN SCOTLAND. THEY ARE INCLUDED TO ASSIST THE VISITOR SELECT HIS/HER HOTEL OR RESTAURANT OF CHOICE. THE AWARDS ARE NOT MANDATORY FOR SELECTION TO THIS PUBLICATION.

PALACE OF HOLYROODHOUSE
Official Residence of Her Majesty The Queen

Best known as the home of Mary, Queen of Scots, the Palace was the setting for many dramatic episodes in her short and turbulent reign.

A visit now includes a special display of the Order of the Thistle, the highest honour in Scotland.

Open daily, except during royal visits.

Enjoy a year's unlimited admission if you purchase your ticket directly from the Palace.

0131 556 5100 www.royalcollection.org.uk

The finest wine glasses for all your senses.

STEVENSONS

SCOTLAND'S
GOOD HOTEL AND FOOD BOOK
2017

HOW TO LOCATE A HOTEL OR RESTAURANT

1. First look at the map of **Scotland on page 12.** The place name of the hotels or restaurants I am featuring will be highlighted in bold type. Restaurants will be highlighted with a red circle. ●

2. Once you have pinpointed your location *follow along the top of the pages*, which are arranged alphabetically, until you arrive at your location.

3. If you already have the name of the hotel or restaurant and wish to know if it is included, turn to the index at the back of the book. Hotels and restaurants are listed alphabetically.

4. In some cases where hotels and restaurants are located close to major towns, they may be shown under that town with the exact location in brackets. For example, **FORT WILLIAM (Torlundy).**

5. **Hotel Price guide:** This quote is based on an overnight stay single & double. Normally this is for bed & breakfast but sometimes if dinner is included it will be indicated. (includes dinner). Also applicable to restaurants with rooms.

MacLeod House & Lodge

6. The above prices are quoted for a one night stay, but most of the establishments in this book offer reductions for stays of two or more nights. Also please enquire about seasonal bargain 'breaks'.

7. **Symbols/Awards.** Awards from VisitScotland (Quality Assurance Classification), AA red food rosettes & stars and the Bull Logo (Scotch Beef Club - Quality Meat Scotland) appear on hotel and restaurant entries. See introductory pages for a full explanation of these symbols and awards.

STEVENSONS

GENERAL NEWS, STAFF APPOINTMENTS & ACTIVITY

Kinnaird House has closed as a Guest House and reverted to a private residence. Estate cottages are still for let. **Paul Leonard** appointed head chef at **Isle of Eriska Hotel, Spa & Island** (formerly with **Andrew Fairlie** at **Gleneagles**). **Cromlix House & Chez Roux** awarded 3 AA food rosettes. **Michael Smith** (ex head chef of **The Three Chimneys**) has opened his own restaurant at Stein on Skye. **Mr. and Mrs. Richard Trevor** have purchased **Eddrachilles Hotel** near Scourie. **Grace Stuart** will be retiring as head housekeeper at **Inver Lodge Hotel** after 29 years. **Fonab Castle & Spa** have appointed **Niall Thompson** as General Manager and **Grant MacNicol** (ex **Rufflets**) as head chef. **The Creel Restaurant** on Orkney has been sold – **Alan and Joyce Craigie** have moved on after 32 years. Michelin star chef **Bruce Sangster (Elie)** has retired!

Fonab Castle Hotel & Spa

NEWSLETTER

MacLeod House & Lodge

Darroch Learg Hotel in Ballater will re-open for business in 2017. **Andrew Turnbull** (ex **Cromlix House**) has been appointed head chef at **Inverlochy Castle**. Head chef **Michael Simpson** celebrates 30 loyal years at **Culloden House**. **The Steadings at the Grouse & Trout** awarded VisitScotland 3 star Gold. **Quinion** family celebrate 42 years at **Farlam Hall** in Cumbria. **63 Tay Street Restaurant** in Perth has had a very attractive refurbishment. **Livingston's Restaurant** in Linlithgow has changed tack to a more bistro offering. **Alex Hay** (ex **Raemoir House**) has joined the kitchen brigade at **Kildrummy Inn**. **Darren Miranda** appointed head chef at **The Horseshoe Restaurant**, near Peebles. **Glencoe House** plan to open 'The Stables' by April 2017. This is a very exciting self catering development which will complement the existing property. No expense has been spared and it will offer total luxury in a secluded environment. **Meldrum House Hotel & Golf Estate** in Aberdeenshire have recently opened their new 28 bedroomed site complete with ballroom.

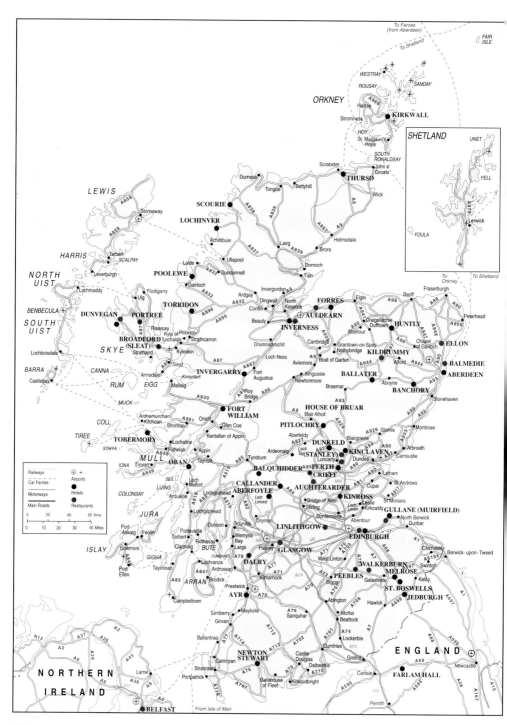

THE MARCLIFFE HOTEL, SPA AND RESTAURANT

North Deeside Road, Aberdeen. AB15 9YA
Tel: 01224 861000   Fax: 01224 868860
Email: reservations@marcliffe.com   www.marcliffe.com

'The Marcliffe Experience' truly reflects the VisitScotland 5 star award but with a personal touch. This theme is prevalent throughout with a 'hands on' approach by the Spence family. I stayed here on six occasions over the last year. The consistently high standards of hotel keeping are obvious and the ambience of the hotel is quite unique. Staff, some of whom I have known for years (and some new faces) are extremely efficient. Bedrooms (suites) are luxurious and the cuisine within the conservatory restaurant outstanding. Afternoon tea a highlight. Public areas exude an atmosphere of warmth with roaring log fires (when required). Menus include Scottish lobster and Russian King Crab and a very good ribeye steak – combined with a very good wine cellar. Gymnasium and beauty spa offering a selection of treatments. A wonderful setting within 11 acres of garden and woodland in the attractive suberb of Cults on the periphery of Aberdeen. Free wi-fi. (First visited 1993).

Open: *All year*	**Gymnasium/Hairdresser/Beauty Spa:** *Selection of treatments*
No. Rooms: *41 En Suite 41*	**Conference Facilities:** *Extremely good*
Room telephones: *Yes*	**Price Guide:** *Single, Double or Twin* **£150.00 - £350.00 (suite)**
TV in Rooms: *Yes*	**Location:** *Aberdeen ring road, turn west at A93 - to*
Pets: *Yes* **Children:** *Yes*	*Braemar. Hotel is 1ml on right.*
Disabled: *Yes*	*Aberdeen airport 25mins.*

RAEMOIR HOUSE HOTEL

Nr. Banchory, Aberdeenshire. AB31 4ED
Tel: 01330 824884
Email: hotel@raemoir.com   www.raemoir.com

This regal Georgian mansion is situated in wide parkland a mile north of Banchory in easy reach of Aberdeen and Royal Deeside. Another most enjoyable overnight stay at this magnificent property described by some as having the 'Downton Abbey' flavour. The approach through the treelined driveway when the 'Rhoddies' are in bloom is most impressive. Part of the house dates from 1715 but the main house was built in 1817. Accommodation comprises 2 luxury suites, 14 superior double rooms and 2 single rooms. Spacious with generous-sized en suite facilities and furnished in the manner befitting a Georgian mansion. The food and beverage operation is quite exceptional. Technical skills and judgement display clear ambition to achieve high standards. Clarity of flavours using good fresh produce from local suppliers from the rich farming and marine harvests of Aberdeenshire. I can assure you that diners' expectations are fully met. There is the option of fine dining or a more informal meal taken in the lounge bar. Great ambience. Service was excellent. Roaring log fires throughout and the comfort of the guest paramount. Conference and wedding enquiries welcome. Your hosts: Mr. and Mrs. Neil Rae. Highly recommended. (First visit, 1992).

Open: *All year*		**Disabled:** *Limited*	
No. Rooms: *18 En Suite 18*		**Conference Facilities:** *60 delegates*	
Room telephones: *Yes*		**Price Guide:** *Single from £125.00*	
TV in Rooms: *Yes*			*Double from £175.00*
Pets: *By arrangement*		**Location:** *Mile north of Banchory*	
Children: *Yes*			

LAKE OF MENTEITH
(HOTEL & WATERFRONT RESTAURANT)
Port of Menteith, Perthshire. FK8 3RA
Tel: 01877 385258
Email: enquiries@lake-hotel.com www.lake-hotel.com

This hotel is situated in the most idyllic and picturesque position one could wish for – right beside the only Lake in Scotland. The 'image' and interior of this hotel have been transformed in recent years. Recent winner of the 'Small Country Hotel' category (Scotland Hotel Awards). Decorated in the warm and welcoming style of a classic New England waterfront hotel, with muted tones and the extensive use of local timber and stone in the restaurant and bar. All rooms have been extensively upgraded with care and attention to detail - rooms with lake views are 'out of this world' with all modern amenities and nice personal touches. In addition to the discerning traveller, the Lake Hotel will provide facilities for exclusive weddings, whilst the food and beverage operation is one of the best in the country. The waterfront restaurant serves excellent seasonal, locally-sourced, produce-based cooking thoughtfully and imaginatively prepared by Head Chef Jamie Crombie. Proprietor Ian Fleming and son Jamie have certainly 'turned' this hotel into a first class operation. Only a short drive from Glasgow or Edinburgh. (First visited, 1989).

Open: *All year*	**Swimming Pool/Health Club:** *No*
No. Rooms: *17*	**Conference Facilities:** *No*
Room telephones: *Yes*	**Price Guide:** *Single from £110.00 Double from £138.00*
TV in Rooms: *Yes*	**Location:** *Turn off M9 at Junct. 10 onto A84, follow to A873*
Pets: *No* **Children:** *Yes*	*signposted Aberfoyle. On to Port of Menteith then*
Disabled: *Yes*	*left down the B8034. Hotel 250 yds on right.*

THE EISENHOWER @ CULZEAN CASTLE
Culzean Castle
Maybole, Ayrshire. KA19 8LE
Tel: 01655 884455 Fax: 01655 884503
email: culzean@nts.org.uk www.eisenhowerculzean.co.uk

Culzean Castle, a National Trust for Scotland property, is located on the west coast of Scotland 12 miles south of Ayr. Its unrivalled position perched on a cliff top, with magnificent sea views, is spectacular. Hidden away at the top of the Castle is The Eisenhower, a country house style hotel, which is available all year round and offers six individually styled rooms and suites. The Eisenhower was once the relaxing retreat of President Eisenhower, having been gifted to him by the Kennedy family. It is now the ideal venue for a relaxing break or a special occasion where you can enjoy all that its location has to offer – close to championship golf courses at Turnberry and Troon. Guests can use the spectacular Round Drawing Room, with fabulous views across to Arran, and the cosy Dining Room, which has views to Ailsa Craig, is ideal for a romantic dinner for 2 or a larger family gathering. For that special gathering the Eisenhower can also be hired for exclusive use to host celebrations including small intimate weddings. Overnight stay here on two occasions - delightful experience. (First visited, 2004).

Open: *All year*	**Swimming Pool/Health Club:** *No*
No. Rooms: *6*	**Conference Facilities:** *Up to 90*
Room telephones: *No*	**Price Guide:** *Single £150.00 – £250.00 Double £225.00 – £375.00*
TV in Rooms: *No*	**Location:** *From Glasgow M77/A77 towards Ayr. Within 1*
Pets: *No* **Children:** *Yes*	*hour of Glasgow airports. Castle is 12 miles south*
Disabled: *Limited*	*of Ayr on A719. Maybole train station 4 miles.*

DARROCH LEARG HOTEL & RESTAURANT

Braemar Road, Ballater, Royal Deeside, Aberdeenshire. AB35 5UX

Tel: 013397 55443

Email: enquiries@darrochlearg.co.uk www.darrochlearg.co.uk

Great news! Pleased to announce that Darroch Learg Hotel will re-open for business in 2017 – check the website for further details. The major restoration work will return this property to its rightful place as a well loved hotel in this beautiful part of Deeside. A permanent and popular fixture in Ballater for many years, Fiona and Nigel Franks have planned the restoration in minute detail – with the comfort of the guest paramount of course. All bedrooms have been refurbished to a high standard as have en suite facilities and a new feature is the lift to all floors. As in the past, there will be a strong emphasis on good food and a good wine cellar. (This reputation has always prevailed here.) Elegance is a word I would use – traits of a more graceful era with the family being an integral part of the experience. Fiona told me that she wanted to retain the ambience that went before – homely with log fires and a place to relax and enjoy. Lovely part of the country with Balmoral just 'up the road' – plenty of hills to climb or follow the whisky and castle trails. Quite unique and highly commended. VisitScotland & AA assessment to follow during 2017. (First Visited 1992)

Open: *All year exc. Xmas & 3 wks Jan.*	**Swimming Pool/Health Club:** *No*
No. Rooms: *12 En Suite 12*	**Conference Facilities:** *12 Director Level*
Room telephones: *Yes*	**Price Guide:** *Double £150.00 - £250.00 (Master)*
TV in Rooms: *Yes*	*Dinner from £40.00*
Pets: *Yes* **Children:** *Yes*	**Location:** *A93 at western end of Ballater on road*
Disabled: *Yes*	*to Braemar*

Timeless Glenfarclas

WHISKY ICONS OF WHISKY
DISTILLER OF THE YEAR

A timeless classic

Consider for a moment our modern world - life passing by with undue haste. Do we sometimes take a wistful look at the decades which have passed?

And yet there are timeless classics which span those decades and capture their essence.

The Glenfarclas 15 and 21 Years Old Single Highland Malts. An expression of history, tradition and independence for the 21st century.

The Spirit of Independence

Glenfarclas encourages responsible drinking.

Visit the Glenfarclas Distillery. For opening times and charges please contact:
Glenfarclas Distillery, Ballindalloch, Banffshire, Scotland AB37 9BD
TEL +44 (0) 1807 500257 **EMAIL** info@glenfarclas.co.uk **WEB** www.glenfarclas.co.uk

MACLEOD HOUSE & LODGE

Trump International Golf Links, Menie Estate, Balmedie, Aberdeenshire. AB23 8YE
Tel: 01358 743300

Email: macleodhouse@trumpgolfscotland.com www.trumpgolfscotland.com

This is a magnificent golfing estate on the north Aberdeenshire coast with wonderful views over the North Sea close to the village of Balmedie. Grounds are immaculate and, cossetted within, you will locate The MacLeod House & Lodge. (Also see front cover and food entry of this book). There are 16 spacious bedrooms with generous en suite facilities (1 on ground level) which are furnished to an extremely high standard and include a mini-bar. In keeping with the VisitScotland 5 star award this property can only be described as luxurious plus. The building, located on an estate dating to the 15th century, has all the attributes of a premier country house. Public areas convey a warm atmosphere – comfort of the guest is paramount. The food and beverage operation is one of the best – whether dining formally at The MacLeod House or the option of the Brasserie at the club house. Head chef Paul Whitecross clearly heads a formidable team. Service was faultless. Ideal base to explore Aberdeenshire, whether it's the Whisky or Castle Trail. Or just a visit to the wildlife sanctuary of the Ythan estuary at Newburgh. Highly recommended.

Open: *All Year*	**Disabled**: *Ground floor room (ramp only)*
No. Rooms: *16*	**Conference Facilities:** *Yes*
Room telephones: *Yes*	**Price Guide:** *Superior B&B £250 (per room)*
TV in Rooms: *Yes*	*Grand Deluxe B&B £350 (per room)*
Pets: *By arrangement*	**Location:** *Just north of Balmedie (Ellon Road) on the*
Children: *Yes*	*A90 out of Aberdeen.*

Scottish
TOURIST BOARD
★★★★★
HOTEL

MONACHYLE MHOR
Balquhidder, Lochearnhead, Perthshire. FK19 8PQ
Tel: 01877 384622 Fax: 01877 384305
Email: info@monachylemhor.com www.monachylemhor.com

If you require a rural and romantic destination allied with comfort, service and excellent cuisine head for Monachyle Mhor at Balquhidder. Only 4 miles from the village itself this property enjoys a spectacular position overlooking Loch Voil and Loch Doine. The estate itself covers 2000 acres and is the domain of Tom Lewis (chef/proprietor) His culinary skills are well known - using fresh produce from the estate or his own organic garden Tom produces dishes which demonstrate complete dedication. Bedrooms are extremely comfortable with all modern amenities. Courtyard cottages with wood burning stoves offer an attractive option, centrally heated with fully equipped kitchen. Mhor 84 (formerly The Kingshouse Hotel, for those of you who can remember!) can be located on the main A84, 9 miles north of Callander. Described as a 'motel' type operation, it has 7 bedrooms which vary in size at an attractive tariff. Food and beverage operation proves popular with passing trade. This is Rob Roy country whose grave can be located in the village of Balquhidder. Member of The Scotch Beef Club. (First visited, 1989).

Open: *All year*	**Disabled:** *Dining only*
No. Rooms: *14 En suite 14*	**Swimming Pool/Health Club:** *No*
Room telephones: *Yes*	**Conference Facilities:** *No*
TV in Rooms: *Yes*	**Price Guide:** *Double £185.00 - £265.00 (suites)*
Pets: *No*	**Location:** *11 mls north of Callander on A84. Turn right at*
Children: *Yes*	*Mhor '84 - 6 mls straight along Glen road.*

ROMAN CAMP COUNTRY HOUSE

Off Main Street, Callander, Perthshire. FK17 8BG
Tel: 01877 330003
Email: mail@romancamphotel.co.uk   www.romancamphotel.co.uk

My association with the Brown family stretches back to Auchterarder House (when it was a hotel) and I am delighted that Eric Brown has penned my main Foreword this year. Roman Camp Country House was originally built in 1625 for the Dukes of Perth as a hunting lodge and this property still retains the aura of a bygone era. Surrounded by magnificent gardens and woodland with strolling peacocks it is a haven of peace and tranquillity. This ambience prevails throughout in the comfort of the public rooms (recently refurbished) with roaring log fires. Each of the 15 bedrooms have their own distinctive theme – spacious and comfortable with nice 'extra touches'. Not many head chefs hold the AA 3 rosette award but Ian McNaught has held this accolade for more years than I care to remember. His technique is brilliant and the flair and imagination comes through in each dish. Well-defined flavours using quality ingredients. Wine cellar of note. Also renowned for their afternoon teas served in the manner that some of us were accustomed to know. (The more mature reader!) An ideal venue for weddings with ample car parking. Just be careful at the entrance from the main street. Hosts Eric and Marion Brown have been here for over 25 years. A warm welcome awaits. Highly recommended. (First visit: 1988).

Open: *All year*	**Swimming Pool/Health Club:** *No*
No. Rooms: *15 En Suite 15*	**Conference Facilities:** *Up to 100*
Room telephones: *Yes*	**Price Guide:** *Single from £110.00 - £210.00*
TV in Rooms: *Yes* **Pets:** *Yes*	*Double from £160.00 - £260.00*
Children: *Yes*	**Location:** *East End of Callander. Main Street from*
Disabled: *Yes*	*Stirling turn left down drive for 300 yards.*

ULLINISH COUNTRY LODGE

Struan, Isle of Skye, Inverness-shire. IV56 8FD
Tel: 01470 572214   Fax: 01470 572341
Email: enquiries@ullinish-country-lodge.co.uk   www.ullinish-country-lodge.co.uk

If you want to 'get away from it all' Ullinish Country Lodge is the ideal place to just 'chill out' as they say now. Classified as a 'restaurant with rooms' this country lodge offers extremely high standards of hotel keeping. I have stayed here on 3 occasions – 4 of the bedrooms are quite spacious and luxurious and 2 are smaller but very snug and cosy. All the extra touches as you would expect from a 5 star establishment. I really like the lounge area with open fire where canapes are served before dinner. Great dinner menu and chef makes good use of local ingredients and there is an emphasis now on seafood which couldn't be more local. From loch & sea to the plate! AA 3 rosette restaurant – expectations are high for this award. AA breakfast award. Exact technique, balance and depth of flavour are important. There can be no doubt that Brian & Pamela Howard have taken this country lodge to a new level. A short distance from Dunvegan Castle (home of The MacLeods) other places to visit are Glenbrittle, Portnalong and Elgol in the south. Staffin & Uig in the north. (First visited, 1949 - with my parents!).

Open: *All year except Jan*	**Swimming Pool/Health Club:** *No*
No. Rooms: *6 En Suite 6*	**Conference Facilities:** *No*
Room telephones: *No*	**Price Guide:** *Single from £90.00*
TV in Rooms: *Yes*	*Double from £130.00*
Pets: *No* **Children:** *Over 16*	**Location:** *9 miles south of Dunvegan on*
Disabled: *Dining only*	*Sligachan Road*

GREYWALLS & CHEZ ROUX

Muirfield, Gullane, East Lothian. EH31 2EG
Tel: 01620 842144   Fax: 01620 842241
Email: enquiries@greywalls.co.uk   www.greywalls.co.uk   www.icmi.co.uk

This is a magnificent country house designed by Sir Edwin Lutyens just 17 miles from Edinburgh. A member of the prestigious Relais & Chateaux it overlooks the famous open championship golf course. The gardens alone are worth a visit. Operated by Inverlochy Castle Management International, Greywalls has become one of the premier hotels in Scotland which will rival any other - the food operation under the direction of the renowned Albert Roux OBE, KFO who is head of the famous cooking dynasty behind such establishments as Le Gavroche which was the first ever restaurant in the UK to be awarded three Michelin Stars is a culinary paradise. French influence obvious and the choice of pike quenelle a pure delight. When I stayed here the bedrooms offered every comfort – spacious and well furnished with excellent en suite facilities. Service and attention to detail could not be faulted. An option here is the Colonel's house which sleeps 8 and offers more privacy. Plenty to do and see in East Lothian including golf! Your host and General Manager: Duncan Fraser. Highly recommended. (First visited, 1994).

Open: *All year*	**Conference Facilities:** *Yes*
No. Rooms: *23*	**Price Guide:** *Single £247.50 - £385.00*
Room telephones: *Yes*	*Double £269.50 - £407.00*
TV in Rooms: *Yes*	*Caddy's Closet (single) £93.50 - £137.50*
Pets: *By request* **Children:** *Yes*	**Location:** *Last turning left after leaving Gullane*
Swimming Pool/Health Club: *No*	*travelling East (N. Berwick).*

RAMNEE HOTEL & RESTAURANT

Victoria Road, Forres, Moray. IV36 3BN
Tel: 01309 672410 Fax: 01309 673392
Email: info@ramneehotel.com www.ramneehotel.com

This fine Edwardian mansion built in 1907 is situated in landscaped gardens to the east of the Royal Burgh of Forres. The Ramnee enjoys a certain amount of isolation but is in easy reach of the town centre which is famous for its parkland floral displays and architectural qualities. Over many years the Ramnee has enjoyed a reputation for consistently high standards of hotel keeping. The bedrooms are a delight, (with 4 poster if required) - elegant, and very comfortable, all with en suite facilities - many have views over the Moray Firth. The cuisine offered at lunch and evening is very traditional and features dishes prepared from the very best of Scotland's larder; guests can choose the informality of the bar or reserve a table in Hamblins Restaurant. There is a friendly atmosphere which radiates throughout the hotel. Golfing is high on the list of sporting activities in this area and businessmen make good use of the conference/seminar facilities. Also see entry for Inverness City Suites. Your host: Garry Dinnes. (First visited, 1989).

Open: *All year.*	**Disabled**: *Dinner only*
No. Rooms: *18 En Suite 18*	**Swimming Pool/Health Club:** *No*
Room telephones: *Yes + WiFi*	**Conference Facilities:** *Theatre up to 100*
TV in Rooms: *Yes*	**Price Guide:** *Single £90.00 - £150.00 Double £100.00 - £170.00*
Pets: *Yes*	**Location:** *A96 Aberdeen-Inverness off by-pass at roundabout*
Children: *Yes*	*to east of Forres - 500 yards on right*

INVERLOCHY CASTLE
(RESTAURANT ALBERT & MICHEL ROUX Jnr. AT INVERLOCHY CASTLE)
Torlundy, Fort William. PH33 6SN
Tel: 01397 702177 Fax: 01397 702953 USA Toll Free Tel: 1-888 424 0106
Email: info@inverlochy.co.uk www.inverlochycastlehotel.com www.icmi.co.uk

A member of the prestigious Relais & Chateaux this is an outstanding castle property set in magnificent landscaped gardens just north of Fort William. It nestles below Ben Nevis in a stunning highland setting. This was my 21st stay at Inverlochy Castle and once again it was the complete experience offering every comfort and quality of service. Without doubt it retains and maintains the finest traditions of hotel keeping. Bedrooms are spacious (especially the 3 main suites) with quality furnishings and décor in keeping with the traditional castle building. The talents of head chef Andrew Turnbull are obvious – high technical skills with flair and imagination. A culinary triumph perfectly executed. In 1873 Queen Victoria described Inverlochy as the most lovely and romantic spot she had seen. I can only agree. The management team under the direction of Jane Watson, who has been here for 36 years, are to be congratulated. A warm welcome, peace and seclusion, with cuisine and wine cellar of the highest order and excellent service. Activities in the area include one of the busiest ski resorts in Scotland. Managed by Inverlochy Castle Management International. (First visited, 1993).

Open: *All year.*		**Swimming Pool/Health Club:** *No*	
No. Rooms: *18*		**Conference Facilities:** *Yes*	
Room telephones: *Yes*		**Price Guide:** *Single £280-£425; Double/Twin £335-£595;*	
TV in Rooms: *Yes*		*Suite £550-£695*	
Pets: *Yes* **Children:** *Yes*		**Location:** *3 miles north of Fort William. In the village*	
Disabled*: Dining only*		*of Torlundy on A82.*	

GOLD

★★★★★

CASTLE HOTEL

Huntly, Aberdeenshire. AB54 4SH
Tel: 01466 792696   Fax: 01466 792641
Email: info@castlehotel.uk.com   www.castlehotel.uk.com

Formerly a home of the Dukes of Gordon this 18th century structure stands in 7 acres of woodland and sweeping lawns in the heart of 'the castle trail' just off the main Aberdeen to Inverness road and a short drive from Aberdeen airport. All bedrooms and suites have been upgraded to a high standard – the suites are particularly spacious and quite luxurious in all aspects. Large en suite facilites. The views from most of rooms and the dining room are spectacular. Enjoy a pre-dinner drink in the aptly named Distillery Bar (this area is part of the whisky trail) and sample traditional Scottish cuisine with fresh produce from the renowned agricultural area of Aberdeenshire, not to mention the marine harvest of its coasts. Truly a family enterprise Andrew & Linda Meiklejohn together with son Stuart and daughter Nikki take an active role with tours organised around this scenic area. Other options could include golf, fishing, trekking or hillwalking. Area steeped in history – an abundance of castles to visit. Service was very courteous and friendly – a very warm welcome and most enjoyable experience. (First visited, 1999).

Open: *All year*	**Swimming Pool/Health Club:** *No*
No. Rooms: *18 En Suite 18*	**Conference Facilities:** *5 up to 50* **Helipad available**
Room telephones: *Free Wi-Fi*	**Price Guide:** *Single £80.00 - £95.00*
TV in Rooms: *Yes*	*Double £125.00 - £175.00 (includes suites)*
Pets: *No* **Children:** *Yes*	**Location:** *Vehicle access via B9022 Portsoy Road,*
Disabled: *Limited*	*off A96*

GLENGARRY CASTLE HOTEL

Invergarry, Inverness-shire. PH35 4HW
Tel: 01809 501254 Fax: 01809 501207
Email: castle@glengarry.net   www.glengarry.net

Glengarry Castle commands a stunning position overlooking Loch Oich between Loch Ness and Loch Lochy in this popular area of Scotland. The ruins of Invergarry Castle, the ancient seat of the McDonnells of Glengarry - which gave shelter to Bonnie Prince Charlie before and after the battle of Culloden stands within sight of the hotel. A real family castle hotel the MacCallum family have been here since 1958 and are rightly proud of their achievements - so many enjoyable visits/overnight stays over a number of years. This Victorian building with grand entrance hall has all the ingredients of that bygone era with large reception and public room areas all with views to the garden and loch. The 26 bedrooms have all the ensuite comforts one would expect, some with four posters. True highland hospitality here with fresh produce being the key to successful traditional cooking - the old fashioned afternoon teas a daily highlight. There are a number of activities to enjoy including walks through extensive woodlands, boating on the loch, fishing and making use of the newly surfaced Elastosol tennis court. Perfect stop over for those travelling to Skye or Inverness and beyond. Your hosts: Donald and Robert MacCallum. (First visited, 1992).

Open: *Mar. 27th - Nov. 6th*	**Swimming Pool/Health Club:** *No*
No. Rooms: *26 En Suite 25*	**Conference Facilities:** *No*
Room telephones: *Yes*	**Price Guide:** *Single £85.00 - £95.00*
TV in Rooms: *Yes*	*Double £125.00 - £230.00*
Pets: *Yes* **Children:** *Yes*	**Location:** *One mile south of Invergarry on A82*
Disabled: *Limited*	*overlooking Loch Oich.*

INVERNESS CITY SUITES
2-7 High Street, Inverness. IV1 1HY
Tel: 01463 715218
Email: stay@invernesscitysuites.co.uk   www.invernesscitysuites.co.uk

Ideally located in the middle of this grand highland city it is a short distance from the River Ness, the castle and the train/bus station. The apartments just exude quality – extremely spacious with bespoke furnishings and all modern amenities one would expect from a 4 star VisitScotland establishment. Lounge, dining and kitchen areas are quite amazing; the master bedrooms are en suite and the second bedroom has it's own bath or shower room. No expense spared here and obviously carefully planned with the comfort of the guest paramount. All apartments have been enhanced with a modern décor and a professional input expressing peace and tranquillity. With improvised planning an apartment can accommodate up to 6 people. Families very welcome. No need for housekeeping duties here – it's all done for you. And if you don't wish to eat 'at home' Inverness is noted for its culinary outlets. All within walking distance. This is a definite 'alternative' type of accommodation which offers all the comforts in a more relaxed (and private) atmosphere. Integral coffee shop. Your host: Garry Dinnes. (Also see separate entry for The Ramnee Hotel in Forres, Morayshire).

Open: *All year.*		**Children:** *Yes*	**Disabled**: *Unsuitable*
No. Rooms: *11 (6 apartments)*		**Swimming Pool/Health Club:** *Treatments can be arranged*	
En suite: *Yes*		**Conference Facilities:** *No*	
Room telephones: *Yes*		**Price Guide:** *1 bedroom apartment £90.00 - £160.00 (seasonal)*	
TV in Rooms: *Yes*		*2 bedroom apartment £160.00 - £270.00 (seasonal)*	
Pets: *By arrangement*		**Location:** *High Street opp. Inverness Town House*	

THE KINGSMILLS HOTEL (INC. THE KINGSCLUB & SPA)

Culcabock Road, Inverness. IV2 3LP
Tel: 01463 257100   Fax: 01463 712984
Email: reservations@kingsmillshotel.com www.kingsmillshotel.com

Perfectly situated on the periphery of Inverness, this hotel caters for the demands of the modern day traveller in all respects. Luxurious accommodation, good food, good leisure facilities, good house-keeping and good service are all mandatory requisites here. The 13 new garden lodges, completed last year, have proved to be a great success and offer a bit of privacy. The Kingsclub Spa which was opened in June 2010 has 37 luxurious bedrooms and 38 bespoke bedrooms were added with the conference centre in 2014. Again regular overnight visits to keep up with everything! The enhancement of this hotel over the years since my first visit in 1978 has been a revelation. The main hotel with swimming pool and gymnasium (free access to guests) still retains the original ethos of an intimate well run urban hotel. Personal touch evident from staff who have been at the hotel for many years. There is a skilled food and beverage operation as one would expect. Buffet breakfast. Corporate and wedding enquiries welcome. Designated events team. A 'feel good factor' prevails throughout. Lift to all floors. 2 designated disabled rooms. General Manager: Craig Ewan. (First visited, 1978).

Open: *All year*	**Swimming Pool/Health Club:** *Yes*
No. Rooms: *147*	**Conference Facilities:** *Up to 450*
Room telephones: *Yes*	*(Various venues. Large & small)*
TV in Rooms: *Yes*	**Price Guide:** *Room rate: £90.00 - £275.00*
Pets: *By arrangement* **Children:** *Yes*	**Location:** *Culcabock Road next to Inverness Golf course.*
Disabled: *2 rooms designated*	*1 mile from city centre.*

Michael Simpson
Head Chef
Culloden House Hotel
(30 years loyal service)

Photograph courtesy of Alan Hunter, Northern Exposures

30 years

CULLODEN HOUSE HOTEL
Culloden, Inverness. IV2 7BZ
Tel: 01463 790461   Fax: 01463 792181
Email: info@cullodenhouse.co.uk   www.cullodenhouse.co.uk

Quite a majestic entrance to this property – a very stately mansion with all the 'trappings' of Bonnie Prince Charlie and the last battle on British soil in April 1746. The sweeping manicured lawns and building-clad virginia creeper cannot fail to impress the visitor and rightly so – the current 'Bonnie Prince Charlie' has been a visitor here of course. Within the elegance and charm of this hotel is true Highland hospitality – guests are met with a genuine welcome – there is a very friendly and relaxed atmosphere which immediately puts you at ease. The 'hands on' approach from General Manager Stephen Davies is quite evident - he seems to be everywhere at the one time! Talented and devoted head chef Michael Simpson (30 years) is known by reputation for his culinary skills and holds the Eat Scotland Silver Award. Bedrooms and ensuite are lavish in their size (rooms 15 and 16 are my favourites) with quality furnishings and every modern amenity. Public areas form the same theme - complete comfort in a quite regal style. The complete experience. Airport 15 minutes. Highly recommended.

Open: *All year*	**Swimming Pool/Health Club:** *No*
No. Rooms: *28 En Suite 28*	**Conference Facilities:** *Up to 40*
Room telephones: *Yes*	**Price Guide:** *Single £175.00 - £365.00*
TV in Rooms: *Yes*	*Double £250.00 - £395.00 (suite)*
Pets: *Yes* **Children:** *Yes*	*Enquire about seasonal breaks*
Disabled: *Not suitable*	**Location:** *3mls from Inverness & 3mls from airport*

For the last 50 years, MORTIMER'S OF GRANTOWN ON SPEY has supplied the best in fishing and outdoor leisure equipment to discerning sports men and women from all over the world.

We stock every conceivable quality accessory including the full range of Hardy fishing tackle and a vast range of equipment from other manufacturers. Most of the leading makes of outdoor clothing for men and women are stocked together with a full range of shooting accessories and ammunition. We even have our own Mortimer's range of single malt and blended whisky. Of course, supplying equipment is only part of our service to you. We are also able to supply fishing permits, from the Strathspey Angling Association, for both banks of a nearby 6 mile stretch of the River Spey. Tuition can be arranged with our experienced ghillies and with the use of the best tackle - hired from us!
    We look forward to meeting you.

MORTIMER'S,
3 HIGH STREET,
GRANTOWN ON SPEY,
MORAY, PH26 3HB.
TEL: 01479 872684.
e-mail: mortimers@spey.fsnet.co.uk
www.mortimersofspeyside.co.uk

THE STEADINGS AT THE GROUSE & TROUT

Flichity, Farr, Inverness-shire. IV2 6XD
Tel: 01808 521314

Email: stay@steadingshotel.co.uk   www.steadingshotel.co.uk

This is a real 'wee gem'. Travel down Strathnairn for 8 miles on the Fort Augustus road (B851) clearly marked from the main A9 just south of Inverness. Another most enjoyable overnight stay in the company of the resident proprietors Mary and David Allen. Formerly a farm steading circa 1860 it is now an extremely well restored and refurbished property. Care has been taken with the 8 en suite bedrooms – all refurbished to a high standard with extra touches. 2 bedroom 'cottages' attached to the hotel itself offer a slightly different option with access to the garden or the gazebo if you want a smoke! Gardens and surrounds are immaculate - and the large conservatory/lounge with newly-installed 'log-burning fire' instills a sense of peace and contentment. Good wholesome cooking here (generous portions I should add) and a real cracking prawn cocktail not seen on many menus these days. Service first class and a real friendly ambience prevails throughout. Game shooting/loch/river/sea fishing available locally. David & Mary extend a real warm welcome to all their guests and its really a 'home from home' atmosphere. Culloden battlefield just up the road – plenty to do and see or just take a wee stroll in the evening. Really good value for money. Favourite room 'Flichity' which is one of the 'cottage bedrooms'. (First visited, 2006).

Open: *March - October*	**Swimming Pool/Health Club:** *No*
No. Rooms: *8 En Suite*	**Conference Facilities:** *Up to 10*
Room telephones: *Yes* **TV in Rooms:** *Yes*	**Price Guide:** *Single £98.00*
Pets: *Yes (by arrangement)*	*Double from £138.00 - £175.00*
Children: *Yes (by arrangement)*	**Location:** *Strathnairn between Farr & Croachy. 5mls*
Disabled: *Yes (dining only)*	*sth of Inverness take B851 to Ft. Augustus.*

Scottish
TOURIST BOARD
★★★
SMALL
HOTEL
GOLD

ALLERTON HOUSE

Oxnam Road, Jedburgh. TD8 6QQ

Tel: 01835 869633

Email: info@allertonhouse.co.uk www.allertonhouse.co.uk

A real 'home from home' would be the best way of describing Allerton House. A very successful operation with a warm welcome from your hosts Christopher and Carol Longden - well known within the hospitality trade. Indeed, well known for their dedication with the comfort of the guest paramount. A stately mansion house with very attractive gardens it commands an elevated position overlooking the Royal Burgh of Jedburgh. There are 6 elegant en suite bedrooms ranging from The Abbey Room on the ground floor (disabled access) to the spacious Queen Mary Suite with 4 poster and views of the garden. Double/twin and single optional. Superior furnishings, linen and drapes extol the virtues of each room. Every modern amenity includes digital TV, ipod docking station, small fridge, hospitality tray and many extras. Also, within the grounds is a small self-catering unit for two people (minimum of a three day stay and price on application). The Macallan lounge with roaring fire offers every comfort – the breakfast is a meal in itself and will last you all day. There are a number of good eating places within the town. Very popular with 'walkers & ramblers' but an opportunity for all who visit the borders of Scotland and also enjoy excellent accommodation at a reasonable cost. Great ambience at Allerton House and a genuine, warm and friendly atmosphere prevails throughout.

Open: *All year*	**Swimming Pool/Health Club:** *Within 5 mins. walk*
No. Rooms: *6 En Suite 6*	**Conference Facilities:** *No*
Room telephones: *No*	**Price Guide:** *Single £60.00 - £75.00*
TV in Rooms: *Yes*	*Double/Twin £85.00 - £95.00*
Pets: *No* **Children:** *Yes*	**Location:** *Edinburgh 50 mls. Turn off A68 opp. Jedburgh*
Disabled: *Yes*	*Abbey into Oxnam Road - 500 yds. on right.*

BALLATHIE HOUSE

Kinclaven, By Stanley, Perthshire. PH1 4QN
Tel: 01250 883268   Fax: 01250 883396
Email address: email@ballathiehousehotel.com   www.ballathiehousehotel.com

This is a magnificent property situated in its own country estate overlooking the River Tay noted for its fishing. The main driveway and garden policies in a woodland setting are immaculate. This house of character dates back to 1850 and is only a short drive from Perth. The main house is simply stunning – bedrooms and public areas all retain that elegance associated with a country house and offer every comfort. I have stayed within the main house and also 'The Riverside Suites'. Exceptional views over the River Tay. There are also the options of 'The Sportsman Lodges' (all en suite) and one self-catering apartment. Sophisticated food and beverage operation here - the technical skills and an ambition to achieve high standards are obvious. The dedication and passion of award winning head chef Scott Scorer is clearly evident in the daily changing menu where he makes the best use of Scottish produce. You will not be disappointed. Ideal venue for weddings. Service and housekeeping could not be faulted. Your host: General Manager: Andrew Seal. Highly recommended. (First visited, 1989).

Open: *All year*	**Swimming Pool/Health Club:** *No*
No. Rooms: *53 En Suite 53*	**Conference Facilities:** *Boardroom meetings to 30*
Room telephones: *Yes*	**Price Guide:** *Single from £60.00 B&B; Double or Twin from*
TV in Rooms: *Yes*	*£100.00 B&B - Special seasonal midweek breaks*
Pets: *Yes* **Children:** *Yes*	**Location:** *Off A9, 2 miles North of Perth through Stanley,*
Disabled: *Yes*	*or off A93 at Beech hedge and signs.*

LYNNFIELD HOTEL & RESTAURANT

Holm Road, St. Ola, Kirkwall. KW15 1SU
Tel: 01856 872505
Email: office@lynnfield.co.uk www.lynnfieldhotel.com

This is now firmly established as a premier destination on the islands of Orkney. Malcolm Stout and Lorna Reid (who moved from Westray in 2006) have taken this property to a new level which is testament to the VisitScotland 4 star rating. Ideal location on the periphery of Kirkwall and next to the Highland Park Distillery. 10 very luxurious bedrooms (including 1 disabled, 3 suites & 2 four posters) – offer every comfort. Their reputation for excellent Orcadian cuisine has followed from Westray, with daily evolving menus. Terrific view over the bay from the restaurant sets the tone for a wonderful dining experience. It's difficult sometimes for me to find a place of this quality on the islands of Scotland – on my visits to Orkney I always found there was plenty to do and see – 3 days to cover visits to Skara Brae, Sheila Fleet Orkney Designer Jewellery, the distillery and a wee drive over The Churchill Barriers or take an evening stroll into the town and do a bit of window shopping. Make sure this one is on your itinerary when planning your trip to Orkney. You will not be disappointed. Highly recommended.

Open: *All year*		**Swimming Pool/Health Club:** *No*	
No. Rooms: *10 En Suite 10*		**Conference Facilities:** *Up to 30*	
Room telephones: *Yes*		**Price Guide:** *Single occupancy from £100.00*	
TV in Rooms: *Yes* **Pets:** *Arrangement*		*Double £125.00 - £165.00 (3 suites)*	
Children: *Over 12*		**Location:** *A961 Holm Road where indicated.*	
Disabled: *1 room*		*Near Highland Park Distillery.*	

Scottish
TOURIST BOARD
★★★★
SMALL
HOTEL

INVER LODGE HOTEL & CHEZ ROUX

Lochinver, Sutherland. IV27 4LU
Tel: 01571 844496   Fax: 01571 844395

Email: stay@inverlodge.com   www.inverlodge.com   www.icmi.co.uk

An outstanding property in a truly highland (and rugged) setting with panoramic views over Lochinver bay. It certainly lived up to its VisitScotland 5 star status during my 2 night stay this year (first visit, 1993). The bespoke Iolaire suite is quite magnificent with its own fireplace but all bedrooms/suites are extremely spacious and comfortable and all have panoramic views over the harbour and beyond. The cuisine (Chez Roux) has taken on a slightly French influence introduced by Albert Roux OBE, KFO who is head of the famous cooking dynasty behind such establishments as Le Gavroche which was the first ever restaurant in the UK to be awarded three Michelin Stars. The abundance of local fresh ingredients, especially fish from the harbour and wild chanterelles, are used in more traditional dishes. The view from the dining room is 'out of this world'. Long-serving General Manager Nicholas Gorton (still here!) and housekeeper Grace Stuart deserve all the plaudits. Sadly, Grace will be retiring after 29 years service at the hotel. She will be missed by us all and we wish her well. Great ambience and comes highly recommended. Managed by Inverlochy Castle Management International. (First visited, 1993).

Open: *Early April-end Oct.*	**Swimming Pool/Health Club:** *No*
No. Rooms: *21*	**Conference Facilities:** *No*
Room telephones: *Yes*	**Price Guide:** *Single £165.00 - £195.00*
TV in Rooms: *Yes*	*Double £250.00 - £530.00*
Pets: *Yes* **Children:** *Yes*	**Location:** *Through village on A835 and turn left after*
Disabled: *Ground floor*	*village hall.*

CLINT LODGE

St. Boswells, Melrose, Roxburghshire. TD6 0DZ

Tel: 01835 822027 Fax: 01835 822656

Email: clintlodge@aol.com www.clintlodge.co.uk

A stunning country house built in 1869 this was formerly a sporting lodge for Lord Polworth and at present owned by the Duke of Sutherland. Now the home of Bill, Heather and daughter Suzie Walker, well known in the local community. Outstanding location above the River Tweed with magnificent views over the border countryside. The lodge has 5 exquisite rooms – all with ensuite/private facilities and furnished to a very high standard in keeping with the period of the house. An added attraction is the 3 bedroomed cottage within the grounds (VisitScotland 4 star) which gives one more options on a self catering basis. Guests can stay on a B/B basis or dinner can be included. Having sampled some of the home baking on my visits I would recommend the evening supper/dinner (optional at £28:50 or £35:00 respectively). Both Heather and Suzie are renowned for their culinary expertise – produce from the rich agricultural border region allied with some terrific homebaking. It's really a home from home with a wonderful conservatory and well furnished public rooms. Nice friendly ambience prevails throughout. Plenty of places to visit including Melrose Abbey and Abbotsford House, home of Sir Walter Scott. Make a note of this one when visiting the borders.

Open: *All Year*	**Conference Facilities:** *Yes + wedding enquiries welcome*
No. Rooms: *5 (4 En Suite); 1 cottage*	**Price Guide:** *Single: from £70; Double: £120.00 - £140.00;*
Room telephones: *WiFi throughout*	*Cottage: POA; Supper: £28.50; Dinner: £35.00*
TV in Rooms: *Yes* **Pets:** *By arrangement*	**Location:** *Turn off A68 onto A6404. Through the village & turn*
Children: *Yes* **Disabled**: *Limited*	*second left just after River Tweed (B6356). Follow through*
Health Club: *No*	*Clintmains, house is on right after approx. 1/2 mile*

KIRROUGHTREE HOUSE

Newton Stewart, Wigtownshire DG8 6AN
Tel: 01671 402141   Fax: 01671 402425
Email: info@kirroughtreehouse.co.uk   www.kirroughtreehouse.co.uk

No doubt one of my favourites in the south west of Scotland with a great core of loyal customers who return year after year. The drive up to the hotel encompasses 8 acres of landscaped gardens which are magnificent, more so when the 'rhodies' are in bloom. This unusual building has been carefully restored and refurbished in keeping with the original house with varying degrees of comfort – from standard, de luxe and the opulent regal suite. All are elegant in their own right – my own room (downstairs) with entrance/exit from the rear and lift to ground floor, was massive. The ensuite facility was as large as a bedroom! The elegant theme continues through to the wood-panelled, extremely comfortable lounge (where you order dinner) and the 2 dining rooms. AA rosetted food offers a la carte dinner from 7.30pm or the option of the bistro, 5-7pm. Great ambience throughout. Service very professional and friendly. Good base for exploring the delights of the south west. Seasonal breaks available. (First visited, 1994).

Open: *Feb 14-Jan 3*	**Disabled:** *Limited*
No. Rooms: *17 En Suite 17*	**Swimming Pool/Health Club:** *No*
Room telephones: *Yes*	**Conference Facilities:** *Max 20*
TV in Rooms: *Yes*	**Price Guide:** *Double from £90.00*
Pets: *By arrangement*	**Location:** *From A75 take A712 New Galloway Road.*
Children: *Over 10*	*Hotel 300 yards on left.*

Paul Leonard
Head Chef - Isle of Eriska Hotel, Spa & Island

ISLE OF ERISKA HOTEL, SPA & ISLAND

Benderloch, By Oban, Argyll. PA37 1SD
Tel: 01631 720371
Email: office@eriska-hotel.co.uk   www.eriska-hotel.co.uk

A fantastic experience once again this year in this 5 star VisitScotland property. A member of the prestigious Relais & Chateaux it upholds the finest traditions of hotel keeping. A majestic Victorian baronial mansion built in 1884, it is situated in 300 acres of mature gardens and woodland policies. Panoramic views over Loch Linnhe and beyond. As an island and spa the activities are numerous – the Buchanan-Smith family have kept pace with the demands of ever changing trends within the industry. The leisure facilities are 'state of the art' with a large swimming pool and beauty treatments. 'Bistro food' available until 7pm. Other activities include golf, biking, clay pigeon shooting or just a game of croquet. There are 5 spa suites, 2 two-bedroom cottages and 3 self-catering units including the 2 hilltop reserves which are quite bespoke. The main hotel retains that elegance of a bygone era. Rooms are luxurious, public rooms spacious with roaring log fires. Dinner was quite a culinary triumph. Head chef Paul Leonard (ex Restaurant Andrew Fairlie) produced a memorable dining experience. Perfectly executed. Service faultless. Unique experience. **(Michelin star awarded 2016-17)**.

Open: *All year*
No. Rooms: *16 Rooms; 9 Suites; 3 self-catering*
Room telephones: *Yes*
TV in Rooms: *Yes*
Pets: *Yes*   **Children:** *Yes*
Disabled: *Yes (2 rooms)*

Swimming Pool/Health Club: *Yes*
Conference Facilities: *By request*
Price Guide: *Rooms £355.00 - £435.00*
Suites £490.00 - £600.00
Location: *Connel Bridge north. Through village of Benderloch. 1 mile beyond turn left (signposted)*

GOLD

THE MANOR HOUSE
Gallanach Road, Oban, Argyll. PA34 4LS
Tel: 01631 562087   Fax: 01631 563053
Email: info@manorhouseoban.com   www.manorhouseoban.com

On the outskirts of Oban just beyond the ferry terminal this Georgian House, built in 1780 commands an enviable position overlooking the Oban bay to the islands beyond. Known to me for many years it is situated in a quiet spot away from the main centre of Oban and retains the charm and elegance of a bygone era. Under the personal supervision of General Manager Gregor MacKinnon, this small hotel offers every comfort one would expect from a VisitScotland 4 star rating and cuisine to match. Bedrooms are extremely comfortable (some with views over the bay), public rooms are spacious, well furnished and cosy with log fire in the winter. The talents of head chef Sean Squire and his kitchen brigade are obvious and over the years this has proved to be a wonderful dining experience. Fresh fish (as one would expect) lamb and game in season could be your choice. Ideal stay for a day journey to the island of Mull or explore the beautiful Argyll coastland north or south of Oban. Breath-taking views from many points along the way. Always an enjoyable stay over a number of years and still a firm favourite. Ideally placed for boarding The Hebridean Princess. (First visited, 1989).

Open: *All year except Christmas*	**Swimming Pool/Health Club:** *No*
No. Rooms: *11 En Suite 11*	**Conference Facilities:** *No*
Room telephones: *Yes*	**Price Guide:** *Single £147.00 – £287.00 (including dinner)*
TV in Rooms: *Yes*	*Double £195.00 – £325.00 (including dinner)*
Pets: *By request* **Children:** *Over 12*	*Enquire about seasonal breaks.*
Disabled: *Restricted*	**Location:** *200yds past ferry terminal on Gallanach Road.*

HEBRIDEAN PRINCESS

Kintail House, Skipton, N. Yorks. BD23 2DE
Tel: 01756 704704   Fax: 01756 704794
Email: reservations@hebridean.co.uk   www.hebridean.co.uk

Sailing mainly from Oban, experience the most beautiful scenery of the British Isles aboard the luxurious Hebridean Princess. This small and unique cruise ship, chartered twice by Queen Elizabeth has immaculately maintained teak decks and polished brass. She cruises Scotland's west coast, Western and Northern Isles in inimitable style. The epitome of understated elegance, from the panoramic Tiree Lounge to the plush Columba Restaurant, the public rooms and 30 spacious cabins are beautifully furnished throughout. Imaginative menus are created using the freshest local produce to bring you memorable breakfasts and elegant dining, with first class service from one of the best crews afloat. Hebridean Princess sails from March until November with a maximum of 50 guests looked after by 38 crew. In addition to cruising her normal waters off Scotland's west coast, including St. Kilda, Northern Ireland and the Isle of Man, Hebridean Princess will cruise the Northern Isles of Orkney and Shetland as well as to Norway in 2017. Hebridean Princess offers fully inclusive cruises of between 4 and 10 nights including all meals, alcoholic and non alcoholic drinks, Internet, transfers and car parking, shore excursions and gratuities on board and ashore.

Open: *From March to November*		**Swimming Pool/Health Club:** *No*	
No. Cabins: *30 En Suite 30*		**Conference Facilities:** *No*	
TV in Cabins: *Yes*		**Price Guide:** *7 nights fully inclusive from*	
Pets: *No*		*£2,630.00 - £10,870 per person*	
Children: *Aged 9 and over*		*Shorter and longer cruises are available*	
Disabled: *Unsuitable*		**Location:** *Argyll*	

TAYCHREGGAN
Kilchrenan, By Taynuilt, Argyll. PA35 1HQ
Tel: 01866 833211/366 Fax: 01866 833244
Email: info@taychregganhotel.co.uk www.taychregganhotel.com

Spectacular position on the banks of Loch Awe with panoramic views surrounded by the rugged mountains of the west highlands. Once a drovers inn it has strong historical connections with Samuel Johnston and James Boswell who stayed here in the 18th century. It is now a fine country house and I spent 2 enjoyable nights here this year. A very romantic and secluded 'hideaway' - the 7 mile single track road from the A85 adds to the sense of occasion (just be careful). Attractive garden and woodland policies and a terrific view over the loch greet you on arrival. Bedrooms from Standard to Master Suite are quite 'de luxe' with very generous en suite facilities. Nice extra touches. Good food and wine are pre-requisites here and the kitchen brigade show a dedication which has earned this hotel 2 AA rosettes for a number of years. Dinner is a 5 course menu priced at £50.00. Wonderful dining room with clothed tables and a terrific view over Loch Awe. Outdoor pursuits here are numerous or you may just wish to climb a mountain or take a leisurely visit to the Oban ferry terminal to Mull. Ideal retreat and wedding enquiries are welcome. Your host for many years: Fiona Sutherland. (First visited 1988 when owned by the Taylor family).

Open: *Closed Nov-April for refurbishment*	**Pets:**	*By arrangement*	
No. Rooms: *18 En Suite 18*	**Swimming Pool/Health Club:** *No (Billiard room)*		
Room telephones: *Yes*	**Price Guide:** *Double £99.00 - £249.00 (master suite)*		
TV in Rooms: *Yes*		*Dinner £50.00*	
Children: *Yes*	**Location:**	*Leave A85 at Taynuilt to B845. 7 mls. through*	
Disabled: *Dining only*		*village of Kilchrennan to lochside*	

AA

THE PARKLANDS HOTEL (& RESTAURANTS)

2 St. Leonard's Bank, Perth. PH2 8EB
Tel: 01738 622451
Email: info@theparklandshotel.com   www.theparklandshotel.com

Celebrating their 13th year at The Parklands in Perth Scott and Penny Edwards have now created a first class 'Boutique City Hotel'. The constant re-investment and upgrading has been exceptional. The hotel is conveniently situated on the periphery of Perth near the railway station and looking out to the South Inch. Attractive gardens and patio area conveys a feeling of 'well-being' and this theme continues throughout the hotel. Luxurious bedrooms with all modern amenities (including business) – bespoke furnishings and a few extra touches. The hotel takes great pride in its food and beverage operation with 'well kent' face Graeme Pallister (Scottish Chef of the Year 2013) at the helm. His team deliver a first class culinary experience – ambience of the dining room adds to the enjoyment. Public rooms extremely comfortable for that pre-dinner refreshment or just for a chat. Very much a 'hands-on' operation which creates a very friendly and comforting atmosphere. Geared up for corporate business seminars or a small wedding. Plenty to do in and around the city: Perth races or Scone Palace could be of interest. Short drive from Edinburgh or Glasgow. (Also, see good food entry for 63 Tay Street). (First visited, 1990).

Open: *All year*
No. Rooms: *15 En Suite 15*
Room telephones: *Yes + Wifi*
TV in Rooms: *Flat screen plasma*
Disabled: *Ground floor rooms/Dining*
Pets: *Yes*   **Children:** *Yes*

Swimming Pool/Health Club: *No*
Conference Facilities: *Up to 24*
Price Guide: *Double £104.00 - £155.00*
Single £94.00 - £129.00 (enquire about seasonal breaks)
Location: *From A90 head towards railway station. Parklands on left at end of South Inch*

AA ❀ ❀

Grant MacNicol
Head Chef - Fonab Castle Hotel & Spa

FONAB CASTLE HOTEL & SPA
Foss Road, Pitlochry, Perthshire. PH16 5ND
Tel: 01796 470140
Email: reservations@fonabcastlehotel.com   www.fonabcastlehotel.com

This is a magnificent Victorian baronial mansion built in the late 1800's by the Sandeman family of Port and Sherry fame. Panoramic views over Loch Faskally and surrounded by attractive woodland and garden policies. Quite a bit of history over the years but eventually bought in 2002 by Jed and Joanne Clark. After a massive refurbishment programme the hotel officially opened in July 2013. No expense has been spared as I was to find out when I stayed here. Befitting the VisitScotland 5 star and 3 AA rosette awards this was quite an outstanding experience. Accommodation is quite luxurious whether staying within the hotel or in one of the 'river lodges'. Bespoke furnishings, spacious rooms and en suite facilities. Also some nice personal touches. Lifts to all floors including the Penthouse. Lodges ideal for families. 'State of the art' Spa with swimming pool, jacuzzi, treatment rooms, sauna, aroma room and steam room. Dinner in the Sandeman Restaurant was a culinary triumph (excellent wine cellar) or there is the option of the award winning brasserie. Ideal venue for weddings or corporate meetings. This is a must for visitors to beautiful Perthshire. Your host: General Manager Niall Thompson. Highly recommended. (First visited, 2016).

Open: *All year*	**Swimming Pool/Health Club:** Yes *(free to guests)*
No. Rooms: *34*	**Conference Facilities:** Yes
Room telephones: Yes; Free Wi-Fi	**Price Guide:** *Single £150.00 - £260.00*
TV in Rooms: Yes	*Double £280.00 - £550.00 (Penthouse)*
Pets: *Lodges only* **Children:** Yes	*(Seasonal breaks available)*
Disabled: Yes	**Location:** *Just off main A9 - signposted Foss Road at Pitlochry.*

AA ❀ ❀ ❀

POOL HOUSE
Poolewe, By Achnasheen, Wester Ross. IV22 2LD
Tel: 01445 781272 Fax: 01445 781403
Email: stay@pool-house.co.uk www.pool-house.co.uk

One of the finest locations in Scotland on the shores of Loch Ewe with panoramic views and a short walk from the famous Inverewe Gardens. Now a Wolsey Lodge offering luxurious accommodation – opulence indeed with quality furnishings and 'nice touches'. Truly a romantic haven, the Harrison family have gone to great lengths to ensure the comfort of the guest. Small and intimate there are 4 massive bedrooms with bespoke en suite facilities. Also, 2 superior self-catering 'cottages' within the grounds. Meals can be arranged by prior arrangement otherwise there are a number of good food outlets in Gairloch (6 miles). I have stayed here 3 times and the experience was superb. This rugged area of Wester Ross attracts many hill walkers – Loch Maree nearby surrounded by towering hills is one of the best in Scotland. Otters and seals abound. A real family run operation for many years and always a warm welcome. Ideal for exclusive use for that special occasion. Quite a unique venue in this isolated yet beautiful part of Wester Ross. **Bookings by phone only - not accepted through a third party.** Your hosts: Peter, Margaret, Elizabeth and Mhairi Harrison. VisitScotland 5 star gold guest house. (First visited, 2000).

Open: *Closed Jan - Feb*	**Swimming Pool/Health Club:** *No*
No. Rooms: *4 suites (+ 2 self-catering)*	**Conference Facilities:** *No*
Room telephones: Yes *(free WiFi)*	**Price Guide:** *Double £325.00; Single £180.00 - £190.00*
TV in Rooms: *Yes*	*Dinner £45.00*
Pets: *By arrangement* **Children:** *Over 16*	*Cottages £1200.00 per week (3&4 day stay available)*
Disabled: *Limited*	**Location:** *Next to Inverewe Gardens.*

Scottish
TOURIST BOARD
★★★★★
GUEST
HOUSE
GOLD

DRYBURGH ABBEY HOTEL

St. Boswells, Melrose, Roxburghshire. TD6 0RQ
Tel: 01835 822261 Fax: 01835 823945
Email: enquiries@dryburgh.co.uk www.dryburgh.co.uk

Nestling in a magnificent wooded private estate on the banks of the River Tweed and immediately adjacent to the historic Dryburgh Abbey, Dryburgh Abbey Hotel commands a stunning position with magnificent views in the heart of the borders. This Scottish baronial mansion dates from the 19th century. Superior bedrooms are spacious, attractively decorated with every comfort one would expect and nice 'extra touches' - some with panoramic views. Large and comfortable bistro area - skilled head chef Mark Wilkinson produces dishes of sound quality with clarity of flavour and, essentially, sources quality produce. Menus vary according to the season. Most enjoyable dining experience and service was excellent. Don't forget the indoor pool - ideal after a day filled with walking, fishing, touring, sporting or just relaxing by the pool itself. This is Sir Walter Scott country, and his home at Abbotsford was opened in 2014 by the Queen after its extensive renovation. The borders is renowned for its agricultural produce and the famous 'Melrose Sevens' rugby tournament. Ideal venue for corporate matters ('away from it all') or weddings - just an hour's drive down the A68 from Edinburgh. Recently awarded 'dog friendly hotel of the year'. Your host: Ken Buchanan. (First visited, 1992).

Open: *All year*	**Disabled:** *Yes*
No. Rooms: *38 (all En Suite)*	**Swimming Pool/Sauna:** *Yes*
Room telephones: *Yes*	**Conference Facilities:** *Yes*
TV in Rooms: *Yes*	**Price Guide:** *£70.00 - £300.00 (Lady of Mertoun Suite)*
Pets: *Yes*	*Enquire about seasonal breaks*
Children: *Yes*	**Location:** *2 miles from St. Boswells, Scottish Borders.*

EDDRACHILLES HOTEL

Badcall Bay, Scourie, Sutherland. IV27 4TH
Tel: 01971 502080

Email: info@eddrachilles.com www.eddrachilles.com

This hotel is superbly situated on Badcall Bay with magnificent views. It was good to return once again to stay and meet 'hands on' resident owners Richard and Fiona Trevor. Formerly a church manse, it has been completely reconfigured and adapted as a 10 en suite bedroomed hotel offering every comfort. No doubt a mecca for wildlife enthusiasts with native otters, seals, roe and red deer. Handa Island nearby is a bird sanctuary and there are many small islands that can be visited by boat. Or just climb a mountain! Excellent home cooking and menus offer a varied choice at a reasonable price. Bedrooms have all been tastefully furnished and have all the amenities required including hospitality tray. Housekeeping was faultless. Comfortable public room areas to relax including the attractive sun porch. Difficult to find a property of this quality in such an isolated area in the far north west of the country. Excellent base for excursions to Durness and Cape Wrath in the north or Ullapool and The Summer Isles to the south. A very scenic and rugged part of Scotland. This is excellent value for money. (First visited, 1992).

Open: *March - October*	**Disabled:** *Limited. Designated parking area.*
No. Rooms: *10 En Suite 10*	**Swimming Pool/Health Club:** *No*
Room telephones: *Yes*	**Conference Facilities:** *No*
TV in Rooms: *Yes*	**Price Guide:** *Single £125.00 (seaview); £100.00 (courtyard)*
Pets: *Yes (dog friendly)*	*Double £165.00 (seaview); £140.00 (courtyard)*
Children: *Yes*	**Location:** *Off A894 - 2 miles south of Scourie.*

FORSS HOUSE HOTEL

Forss, By Thurso, Caithness. KW14 7XY
Tel: 01847 861201 Fax: 01847 861301
Email: anne@forsshousehotel.co.uk www.forsshousehotel.co.uk

Forss House nestles in 20 acres of woodland beside a picturesque water mill just 4 miles outside Thurso. Overnight visits for the past 18 years have witnessed great progress at this property. All bedrooms in the main hotel have been furnished to an extremely high standard - a professional input apparent with quality furnishings and fabrics with the comfort of the guest enhanced by the newly installed biomass system. There are 4 de-luxe bedrooms within the grounds of the hotel - suit the slightly disabled with parking at your front door. Dedication of head chef Andrew Manson and his brigade was very evident here on my visit. Clear ambition to achieve high standards with a bit of innovation - seasonal fresh produce and well-defined flavours. Meal perfectly executed. Breakfast taken in an attractive conservatory setting (9am deadline!). Great ambience from the pre-dinner drink through to the coffee. Cocktail bar boasts over 300 malts and there is a function suite that can take up to 14 for private dinners etc. Gills Bay ferry to Orkney is 'just down the road' as is John O'Groats and Castle of Mey, Plenty to do here – stay a bit longer this time and enjoy. Your host of many years and well known to all: Anne Mackenzie. (First visited, 1998).

Open: *All year (closed 23rd Dec – 4th Jan)*	**Disabled:** *Limited*
No. Rooms: *14 En Suite 14*	**Swimming Pool/Health Club:** *No*
Room telephones: *Yes*	**Conference Facilities:** *Up to 20*
TV in Rooms: *Yes*	**Price Guide:** *Single from £100.00 - £135.00*
Pets: *Yes*	*Double from £135.00 - £185.00*
Children: *Yes*	**Location:** *4 miles from Thurso on A836*

AA ❀ ❀

HIGHLAND COTTAGE

Breadalbane Street, Tobermory, Isle of Mull, Argyll PA75 6PD
Tel: 01688 302030
Email: davidandjo@highlandcottage.co.uk www.highlandcottage.co.uk

Proprietors Jo' and David Currie were poised for retirement but due to popular demand decided to carry on trading. Highland Cottage is a small converted street cottage overlooking Tobermory Bay and away from the main 'hustle & bustle' of the main tourist area. With only 6 delightful bedrooms there is an intimate 'feel' that permutates throughout with a warm welcome from David who handles 'front of house' and Jo' who works miracles in the kitchen. Now operating on a 'full-time' basis for residents (non-residents only by prior reservation), menus are varied with good choice that reflects the 2 AA rosette award. Dedicated approach and exceptional culinary skills – perfect dining experience when I stayed here on 2 occasions. Bedrooms offer every comfort with quality furnishings, every amenity and named after Scottish islands. A 'home from home' atmosphere prevails with every comfort. Things to do abound with a trip to Iona, a visit to Duart Castle (MacLean Clan Chief) or whatever you fancy. Ferry crossing from Oban to Craignure. (First visited, 2002).

Open: *All year ex. Mid Oct-Mid Nov Restricted Opening Jan-Feb*	**Swimming Pool/Health Club:** *No*
No. Rooms: *6 En Suite 6*	**Conference Facilities:** *Small board meetings*
Room telephones: *Yes + Free WiFi*	**Price Guide:** *Double from £140.00 - £170.00 (single on request)*
TV in Rooms: *Yes*	*Dinner £42.50*
Pets: *Yes* **Children:** *Over 10*	**Location:** *Roundabout at top of town – straight across then first right into Breadalbane Street*
Disabled: *Yes Cat. 1 STB*	

THE TORRIDON
Torridon, Wester Ross. IV22 2EY
Tel: 01445 791242
Email: info@thetorridon.com www.thetorridon.com

An outstanding Victorian baronial mansion in a spectacular setting with panoramic views over Loch Torridon to the mountains beyond. Whether approaching from Kyle of Lochalsh or Kinlochewe this is one of the most beautiful areas of north west Scotland. In 1992 the Gregory family moved from Kinlochbervie Hotel to Torridon and undertook a massive overhaul of the building. It now ranks as one of the premier destinations in the country. Opulence abounds with luxury spacious bedrooms (classic to master suites) and public rooms offer every comfort – welcoming log fire in the main reception hall quite a feature. The food here is quite exceptional. This is a highly-skilled operation led by head chef David Barnett. Diners expectations fully met. AA 3 rosette award demonstrates the dedication of the kitchen brigade. The Torridon Inn nearby provides the option to dine in a more informal setting. Now known as an activity destination there are various pursuits to cover most requests. Corporate enquiries welcome and maybe even a small wedding. Voted AA Scottish Hotel of the Year (2012-2013). Yours hosts Rohaise (née Gregory) and Daniel Rose-Bristow. (First visited, 1993).

Open: *All year ex. 4 weeks January*	**Swimming Pool/Health Club:** *No*
No. Rooms: *18 En Suite 18*	**Conference Facilities:** *16 Director level*
Room telephones: *Yes*	**Price Guide:** *Double £245.00 - £510.00 (includes dinner)*
TV in Rooms: *Yes*	*Tariff depends on season & length of stay.*
Pets: *Yes - in cottage* **Children:** *Yes*	**Location:** *Inverness - Achnasheen. Take A832 to Kinlochewe*
Disabled: *Yes*	*village. Take turning clearly marked Torridon 10 miles.*

FARLAM HALL

Brampton, Cumbria. CA8 2NG
Tel: 016977 46234   Fax: 016977 46683
Email: farlam@farlamhall.co.uk   www.farlamhall.co.uk

This is truly a magnificent 17th century ivy clad country manor set amongst wonderful parkland – a member of the prestigious Relais & Chateaux no less. The lake and fountain to the front are remarkable features – from the moment you arrive and enter Farlam Hall there is an atmosphere of peace and contentment. A stroll in the gardens with afternoon tea sets the tone – bedrooms are extremely comfortable – spacious (large windows) and well furnished complimented by large en suite bathrooms. This was my 12th overnight stay at Farlam Hall - a most enjoyable experience on every occasion. The option of the new 2 bedroomed Laundry Cottage (self-catering) within the grounds is proving to be a great success (POA). The **3 AA red star** award indicates the comfort of the guest is paramount here. Add to this the fine cuisine and attentive service and you have the complete product. Daily-changing menus - a great dining experience. All fresh ingredients, carefully sourced and so well executed by chef Barry Quinion. Home made desserts 'to die for'. Just 'over the border' this is an ideal stop whether travelling north or south. Hadrian's Wall and many other historical sites closeby. Go for it, indulge yourself. A real homely atmosphere which the Quinion family have carefully nourished over a 42 year period. (First visited, 2003).

Open: *All year ex. 24th-30th Dec; 8th-26th Jan*	**Swimming Pool/Health Club:** *No*
No. Rooms: *12 En Suite 12*	**Conference Facilities:** *Up to 12 director level*
Room telephones: *Yes*	**Price Guide:** *Single £165.00 - £195.00 dinner, b&b*
TV in Rooms: *Yes*	*Double £310.00 - £370.00 dinner, b&b*
Pets: *Yes* **Children:** *Over 5*	**Location:** *Junction 43 on M6. 12 miles on A689 to*
Disabled: *Not suitable*	*Alston. Not in Farlam village.*

AA ★★★

MALLORY COURT

Harbury Lane, Leamington Spa, Warwickshire. CV33 9QB
Tel: 01926 330214   Fax: 01926 415714

email: reception@mallory.co.uk   www.mallory.co.uk

Mallory Court Hotel is a breathtakingly beautiful country house hotel, set in 10 acres of gardens and just outside Leamington Spa, Warwickshire. A member of the prestigious Relais & Chateaux group it has already been recognised by the AA as one of their top hotels in the country. Formerly head chef at Inverlochy Castle, Simon Haighe has now become Food and Beverage Director and has overall control of the Eden Collection of which Mallory Court is a member. The 3 AA rosette award has been held for many years and the Brasserie now holds a 2 AA rosette award. Consistent and all dishes perfectly executed. No disappointments and diners' expectations fully met. This elegant, Lutyens-style country manor house is quite the little piece of England; an idyllic, impeccable retreat set in 10 acres of landscaped grounds and immaculate lawns. Contemporary country house splendour is the style, where pampered relaxation comes easy in sumptuous lounges over aperitifs or coffee, the mellow, homely atmosphere cultivated by an efficient, dedicated and enthusiastic team. Certainly appeals to the more discerning traveller. Highly recommended.

Open: *All year*	**Disabled:** *2 rooms*
No. Rooms: *31*	**Swimming Pool/Health Club:** *Yes*
Room telephones: *Yes*	**Conference Facilities:** *Excellent - up to 160*
TV in Rooms: *Yes*	**Price Guide:** *£180.00 - £550.00*
Pets: *Arrangement*	**Location:** *M40 from London, Jct. 13; from Birmingham*
Children: *Yes*	*Jct. 14. 2 mls. on B4087 to Leamington Spa.*

AA❀ ❀ ❀

★★★

MARLFIELD HOUSE

Gorey, Co. Wexford, Ireland.
Tel: (00353) 5394 21124   Fax: (00353) 5394 21572
Email: info@marlfieldhouse.ie   www.marlfieldhouse.com

Once again I am delighted to include Marlfield House as my Irish 'Associate Hotel' for edition 2017. It came strongly recommended and is a member of the prestigious Relais & Chateaux group. Formerly the residence of the Earls of Courtown Marlfield House is a very elegant 19th. century mansion set in its own grounds of wonderful garden, woodland and parkland policies. The State Rooms are decorated with rich fabrics and fine antique furniture - all have period marble fireplaces and elegant marble bathrooms. Every room is spacious and offers every luxury. The interior of the hotel is resplendent with fine paintings and antiques and the conservatory is a feature overlooking the garden. Cuisine described as 'classical with a French and Mediterranean influence' which has been awarded 2 AA red rosettes for food. New concept opened this year is The Duck Terraced Restaurant where food is available all day (Bistro style). The Bowe family are to be congratulated on keeping the standards of yesterday today. To maintain such high standards is testament to a firm commitment and dedication. Relais & Chateaux member since 1984. 3 AA red stars. Your hosts: the Bowe family.

Open: *All year exc. Jan 2nd - mid Feb.*	**Disabled:** *Limited*
No. Rooms: *13 rooms; 6 suites*	**Swimming Pool/Health Club:** *No*
Room telephones: *Yes*	**Conference Facilities:** *Small - Director Level*
TV in Rooms: *Yes*	**Price Guide:** *Double. Room - Standard:* ***Euro 260 - 295***
Pets: *Arrangement*	*State Rooms:* ***Euro 405 - 790 (Master)***
Children: *Yes*	**Location:** *80 km south of Dublin*

AA❀❀
★★★

YNYSHIR HALL

Eglwysfach, Machynlleth, Powys, SY20 8TA

Tel: 01654 781209   Fax: 01654 781366

email: info@ynyshir-hall.co.uk   www.ynyshir-hall.co.uk

Another member of the prestigious Relais & Chateaux (since 2001) this is certainly one for the connoisseur. Delightful 16th century manor house surrounded by magnificent gardens - opulence and gracious living on a fine scale - the perfect 'hideaway' in the west of Wales near Aberwyswyth. The 9 bedrooms which include 2 suites are perfectly appointed - large with antique beds and furniture to complement. The regular input since 1989 by owner and renowned artist Rob Reen is quite evident. Interiors express warmth, elegance and charm. The **Michelin Star** and 4 AA red rosette award for food demonstrates a high commitment in achieving high standards of cuisine using high quality suppliers with fresh seasonal produce. Excellent technical skills successfully executed. Cocktail bar with log fire and restaurant with fine linen and glassware allied with an excellent wine list is the complete dining experience **(Michelin Star awarded 25/9/14)**. Ideal location for a visit to the Dovey estuary - one of the finest bird reserves in the country. AA Hotel of the Year for Wales 2014-2015.

Open: *All year*	**Disabled:** *1 room*
No. Rooms: *5 rooms; 5 suites*	**Swimming Pool/Health Club:** *No*
Room telephones: *Yes*	**Conference Facilities:** *Director level 25*
TV in Rooms: *Yes*	**Price Guide:** *Double £230.00 - £550.00*
Pets: *1 room only*	*Suites £230.00 - £705.00*
Children: *Over 9*	**Location:** *10 miles from Aberwystwyth.*

AA ❀❀❀❀
★★★★

STEVENSONS

SCOTLAND'S
GOOD FOOD BOOK WITH RECIPES
2017

Photo by kind permission of Eat on the Green, Udny, Aberdeenshire

STEVENSONS

SCOTLAND'S GOOD FOOD BOOK
2017

FOREWORD

Eat on the Green is honoured to once again, be part of the STEVENSONS GOOD HOTEL AND FOOD BOOK.

Since we opened Eat on the Green twelve years ago, Alan has become a trusted friend who has seen our business grow and flourish. Being part of the STEVENSONS GUIDE has helped put Eat on the Green on the map, bringing visitors from far and wide to Udny Green.

We offer 'something rather special' creating dishes using the finest local produce, attentive service and a welcoming atmosphere. Good food is at the heart of everything we do and we work closely with a handpicked list of suppliers, who share our ethos and passion for delivering high quality produce. The restaurant has recently been refurbished to a very high standard and it is also home to The Laurent Perrier Champagne Lounge, the first of its kind in Scotland.

Now in its 22nd year, the establishments included in the STEVENSONS GUIDE are handpicked by Alan. He takes the time to get to know the businesses he features, building up a relationship and understanding what they are all about. It is this approach which makes the STEVENSONS GUIDE truly unique, and one of the most reliable, and honest guides to the best food and drink in Scotland.

Craig Wilson
Proprietor/Chef
Eat on the Green
Udny
Aberdeenshire

Craig Wilson - Proprietor/Chef
Eat on the Green Restaurant
Udny, Aberdeenshire

Tea & Coffee Solutions

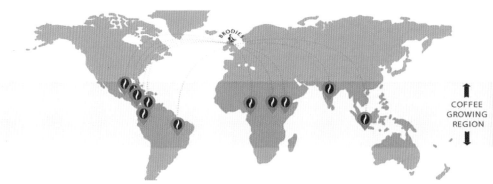

COFFEE
GROWING
REGION

Brodies offers a fully integrated tea and coffee solution. From our fine tea selection blended from around the world and coffee roasted daily by hand, to our comprehensive range of coffee machines and hospitality products, we have it all. Buying Brodies is only the start of the experience, we pride ourselves in our continuing customer service and ongoing Barista training programme.

Brodie Melrose Drysdale & Co Ltd.
Newhailes Industrial Estate, Newhailes Road, Musselburgh, EH21 6SY.
T: 0131 653 4010 F: 0131 653 4020
sales@brodies1867.co.uk www.brodies1867.co.uk

THE CONSERVATORY
(THE MARCLIFFE HOTEL, SPA AND RESTAURANT)
North Deeside Road, Aberdeen. AB15 9YA
Tel: 01224 861000   Fax: 01224 868860
Email: reservations@marcliffe.com   www.marcliffe.com

The Conservatory Restaurant is an integral part of The Marcliffe Hotel in Aberdeen and operates a first class food and beverage operation. I have dined here on many a occasion over the years – as the name suggests the large conservatory area has been designed to offer maximum comfort. Elegantly furnished with clothed tables and wonderful service. Seasonal menus (a la carte) include fish, meat and game dishes. Seafood (crab and lobster) a speciality. Quality suppliers as indicated on the menus. Dedication of the kitchen brigade under the direction of head chef Ross Spence is obvious. Diners expectations fully met. Great wine cellar. An outstanding breakfast here marked at 10/10. Great ambience. Ideal for that special occasion in perfect surroundings. Aberdeen airport 25 minutes. Ample car parking.

Open: *All year*	**Disabled:**	*Yes*
No Rooms: *42 ensuite*	**Price Guide:**	*Same a la carte menu for lunch*
TV in Rooms: *Yes*		*and dinner £25.00 - £65.00*
Room Tel. *Yes*	**Location:**	*Aberdeen ring road. Turn west at A93*
Children: *Yes*		*to Braemar. 1 mile on right*

KILDRUMMY INN
Kildrummy, Alford, Aberdeenshire. AB33 8QS
Tel: 019755 71227
Email: enquiries@kildrummyinn.co.uk   www.kildrummyinn.co.uk

Another most enjoyable overnight stay at this secluded but attractive location in Strathdon, not far from Alford. Operated by Master Chef of Great Britain David Littlewood and his brother-in-law Nigel Hake, it is enjoying the plaudits of many from far and wide. A very skilful food operation with a dedicated approach, sound technical skills using seasonal quality produce. Clear and well-defined flavours - meal perfectly executed. Chantarelles and other foraging on your doorstep. Nigel on hand to advise on a very good wine cellar. The country inn ambience is prevalent – a relaxed, comfortable and friendly atmosphere but with seriously good food. The Inn even has a private fishing beat on the salmon and trout-rich River Don. There are 4 miles of fishing rights and 20 pools – the area is renowned for its 'hunting, stalking and fishing'. There are 4 very comfortable en suite bedrooms. Designated area for private functions. Ideal base to explore and enjoy the wonderful undulating scenery of Strathdon and Strathbogie. AA

Open: *All year ex. Jan. & Tuesdays*	**Disabled:**	*Dining only*
No Rooms: *4*	**Covers:**	*40*
TV in Rooms: *Yes*	**Price Guide:**	*Dinner £28.00 - £35.00*
Room Tel. *No*	**Location:**	*Just before Kildrummy Castle on*
Children: *Yes*		*A97 from Alford*

Andrew Fairlie
Restaurant Andrew Fairlie
Gleneagles Hotel

RESTAURANT ANDREW FAIRLIE

The Gleneagles Hotel, Auchterarder, Perthshire. PH3 1NF
Tel: 01764 694267 Fax: 01764 694163.
Email: reservations@andrewfairlie.co.uk www.andrewfairlie.com

A household name, Andrew Fairlie has achieved the ultimate dining experience. He is driven by innovation, evolving ideas and new concepts and his technical skills are obvious. Located at the iconic Gleneagles Hotel, in this beautiful part of Perthshire, my 14th visit was once again the complete dining experience. Style of cooking can be described as classical French with a contemporary twist. Sophisticated menus (a la carte, du Marche and degustation) with carefully sourced ingredients from moor and glen, local farms and fresh produce from the well-developed walled garden. Great ambience and a very fine wine cellar. The front of house operation under the direction of 'well kent face' Dale Dewsbury is one of the best. This is one for the connoisseur. Multi awarded restaurant with **2 Michelin Stars** and 4 AA rosettes. A wonderful testimonial for the Scottish culinary industry. (First visited, 2003). *AA*❀❀❀❀ 🐽

Open: *All year (Dinner only) ex 3wks Jan. Closed Sun.*		**Disabled:**	*Unsuitable*
No Rooms: *N/A*		**Covers:**	*56*
TV in Rooms: *N/A*		**Price Guide:**	*£95.00 - £125.00*
Room Tel. *N/A*		**Location:**	*Ground floor of Gleneagles Hotel.*
Children: *Over 12*			

AULDEARN *(Nairn)*

BOATH HOUSE

Auldearn, Nairn. IV12 5TE
Tel: 01667 454896
Email: info@boath-house.com www.boath-house.com

This has been 'home' to head chef Charlie Lockley for the past 18 years. No compromise here – cuisine which demonstrates a thorough grounding in classical techniques and equally at ease with modern or traditional dishes. Innovation with an element of excitement and all items made in house. Knows all his suppliers on a personal basis and only quality ingredients are used – foraged food such as herbs, fruit, wild garlic and chanterelles are mandatory. Superior wine cellar to complement a fine dining experience – perfectly executed. Most attractive dining area which overlooks the manicured lawns and garden policies. Front of house staff show that professional attitude – efficient but extremely friendly. The award of 4 AA rosettes and a **Michelin Star** is true testament to a lot of hard work by Charlie Lockley and his kitchen brigade. Your hosts: Don & Wendy Matheson. *AA* ❀ ❀ ❀ ❀ 🐽

Open: *All year*		**Covers:**	*28*
No Rooms: *8*		**Price Guide:**	*Dinner: £45.00 (3 courses) - £70.00 (6 courses)*
TV in Rooms: *Yes*	**Room Tel.** *Yes*		*Lunch: £24.00 (2 courses) - £30.00 (3 courses)*
Children: *Yes*		**Location:**	*1 mile east of Nairn on main Inverness -*
Disabled: *1 Room*			*Aberdeen road.*

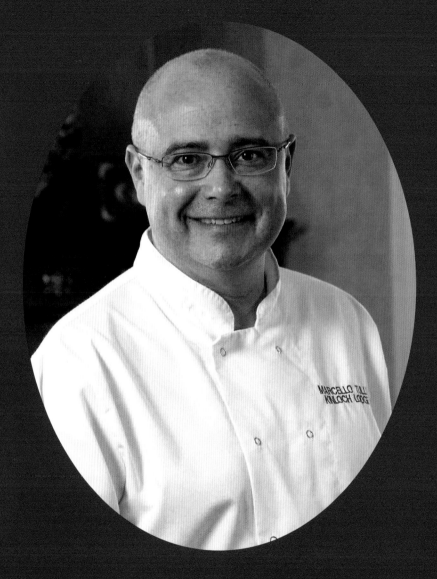

Marcello Tully
Director/Head Chef - Kinloch Lodge
Isle of Skye

BALMEDIE *(Aberdeenshire)*

MACLEOD HOUSE RESTAURANT

Trump International Golf Links, Menie Estate, Balmedie, Aberdeenshire. AB23 8YE

Tel: 01358 743300

Email: macleodhouse@trumpgolfscotland.com www.trumpgolfscotland.com

Magnificent parkland setting with manicured lawns sets the tone as you drive down to the MacLeod House Restaurant just north of Balmedie on the periphery of Aberdeen. Distinct feeling of opulence on the approach but a very friendly and professional greeting on arrival. Known by reputation, head chef Paul Whitecross delivers a gastronomic delight using all his experience with dishes using well known suppliers to create well-balanced menus from local produce. Dishes may include Cullen Skink, Highland venison, scorched cod fillet and a hot mango soufflé, coconut and vanilla bean sorbet. Extremely comfortable table settings and service was faultless. Although there are 16 luxurious bedrooms the restaurant is open to non-residents and private dining is also available. No doubt it is gaining a reputation as a food destination alongside the famous golf links. Corporate and wedding enquiries welcome. (Also see hotel entry).

Open: *All year*	**Covers:**	*48*
No. Rooms: 16	**Price Guide:**	*Sunday lunch £29.50 - £39.50*
TV in Rooms: *Yes*		*Dinner £37.50 - £49.00*
Room Tel. *Yes*	**Location:**	*Just north of Balmedie (Ellon Road)*
Disabled: *Ground floor room (ramp only)*		*on the A90 out of Aberdeen*

BROADFORD *(Sleat, Isle of Skye)*

KINLOCH LODGE

Sleat, Isle of Skye, Inverness-shire. IV43 8QY

Tel: 01471 833333 Fax: 01471 833277

Email: reservations@kinloch-lodge.co.uk www.kinloch-lodge.co.uk

Outstanding property situated on the south of the island (Sleat) with magnificent views over Knoydart. Annual visit this year was in April to meet up again with award winning chef Marcello Tully and enjoy another wonderful dining experience. All dishes perfectly executed from tasty canapes through to petit fours. High expectations fully met. Wine cellar of note and great ambience. Marcello's kitchen workshop is now an integral part of the operation and is proving to be a great success - residential and non-residential guests can now enjoy dinner in Marcello's Chef's table which sits 4 and looks directly into the kitchen – fascinating for those interested in the workings of a **Michelin Star** kitchen. All bedrooms are luxurious, spacious with generous en suite facilities (2 master suites). All furnished to a high standard. The home of Lady Claire Macdonald and Lord Godfrey the lodge is now run by their daughter Isabella and Marcello who are co-directors. Designated disabled facilities with preferential parking and ramp and now a new helipad for guests' convenience. **Michelin Star** and 3 AA rosettes. Highly recommended. (First visited, 1991).

Open: *All year*	**Price Guide:**	*Lunch £36.00 - £39.00 (2 or 3 courses)*
No Rooms: *19 ensuite*		*Dinner £75.00*
TV in Rooms: *Yes* **Room Tel.** *Yes*		*Tasting menu £85.00*
Children: *Yes*	**Location:**	*Short distance from Broadford on the*
Disabled: *Yes - 3 rooms* **Covers:** *50*		*Armadale Ferry road*

Scottish quality salmon

Quality Approved
SCOTTISH
SALMON

Naturally they're the best

www.scottishsalmon.co.uk

BARLEY BREE

6, Willoughby Street, Muthill, Nr. Crieff, Perthshire. PH5 2AB

Tel: 01764 681451

Email: info@barleybree.com www.barleybree.com

More improvements here - the dining area has been enlarged and the bar area moved through to the lounge. Also, new flooring has been installed. Wise investment by owners Alison and Fabrice Bouteloup who have developed this restaurant as a premier food destination. Lovely rural 'village' location not far from Crieff/Auchterarder. Just be careful at the entrance through an archway from the main road. There are 6 extremely comfortable bedrooms which exude quality and have earned them a 4 star Gold VisitScotland rating (Restaurant with Rooms). The 'rustic' themed dining room is a delight and Fabrice produces dishes (with some innovation) which clearly shows dedication and sound technical skills – consistent with well defined flavours. Over the years this restaurant with rooms has received a plethora of awards, with more to follow, no doubt. Very professional 'front of house' and service could not be faulted. Garden area to the rear of the property which is also the entrance to the restaurant and rooms. A 'must visit' on your itinerary. 🐷

Open: *Refer to website (family commitments!)*	**Price Guide:**	*Rooms £110.00 - £150.00*
No Rooms: *6 En Suite 6*		*Lunch £22.50*
TV in Rooms: *Yes* **Room Tel.** *No*		*Dinner £35.00 - £40.00*
Disabled: *Unsuitable*	**Location:**	*Main Street, Muthill - caution at*
Children: *Yes*		*entrance through archway*

BRAIDWOODS

Drumastle Mill Cottage, By Dalry, Ayrshire, KA24 4LN

Tel: 01294 833544 Fax: 01294 833553

email: keithbraidwood@btconnect.com www.braidwoods.co.uk

Michelin Star restaurant since 2000 Keith and Nicola Braidwood fully deserve the plaudits they have received over the years. Attractive converted country styled cottage surrounded by fields just outside Dalry in Ayrshire. Idyllic situation. I have known Keith and Nicola since their days at Shieldhill Country House near Biggar where their culinary efforts were also recognised. By repute expectations are high and I have never been disappointed when sampling the fayre. Great prep work and good sourcing of ingredients are obvious. High technical skills here with flair and a consistency throughout the meal. Depth of flavour evident. No restricted menu here – sophisticated and varied choice. Boneless quail stuffed with black pudding a favourite. Nicola's 'front of house' skills are exemplary – relaxed atmosphere and a warm welcome. Too many awards to mention – Highly commended. Keith and Nicola are both Masterchefs of Great Britain. (First visited, 2000).

Open: *All year ex 3wks Jan & 2wks Sept*	**Price Guide:**	*Lunch £25.00-£28.00 (2 or 3 Course)*
Closed Sun dinner, Mon all day, Tues lunch		*Dinner £48.00-£52.00 (3 or 4 course)*
Children: *Over 12*		*Sunday lunch £32.00 (May - September)*
Disabled: *Not suitable*	**Location:**	*Take road to Salcoats from A737 - 1 mile*
Covers: *24*		*and follow signs.*

Jeff Bland - Executive Chef
Number One Restaurant
The Balmoral Hotel, Edinburgh

THE THREE CHIMNEYS
AND THE HOUSE OVER-BY
Colbost, By Dunvegan, Isle of Skye. IV55 8ZT
Tel: 01470 511258   Fax: 01470 511358
Email: eatandstay@threechimneys.co.uk   www.threechimneys.co.uk

Winner of numerous awards, Shirley and Eddie Spears have forged an oasis of culinary excellence, in the middle of nowhere, which began with the renovation of the 100 year old cottage some 30 years ago. The consistency in the standard of cuisine over the years has been extraordinary. With the introduction of 6 suites in 1999 it took on a 'new look' – and developed into a 5 star VisitScotland 'Restaurant with Rooms'. De luxe suites with small verandah and panoramic views over Loch Dunvegan. Only a short distance from Dunvegan itself the area is abundant in natural food resources – fresh fish, game, lamb and venison – seafood a speciality. There was a distinct improvement this year - head chef Scott Davies has certainly 'settled in' well and the 'front of house' operation was first class. Dedication and complete commitment by the kitchen brigade and diners' expectations are fully met. Only 4 miles from Dunvegan on road to Glendale under the watchful eye of 'The Macleod Tables'. (First visited, 1991). *AA* 🏵🏵🏵 🍴

Open: *All year (ex. 2 weeks Jan)*		**Disabled:** *Yes*	
No Rooms: *6 Suites*		**Price Guide:** *Lunch £38.00 - £55.00 Dinner £65.00 (3 courses)*	
TV in Rooms: *Yes*		*Tasting Menu £90.00 (7 courses)*	
Room Tel. *Yes*		**Location:** *B884, 4 miles West of Dunvegan on*	
Children: *Yes*		*Road to Glendale*	

NUMBER ONE RESTAURANT
1, Princes Street, Edinburgh. EH2 2EQ
Tel : 0131 557 6727   Fax : 0131 557 3747
Email : numberone@thebalmoralhotel.com   www.roccofortehotels.com

Dinner at Number One is indeed a wonderful dining experience. One for 'the foodies' of that there is no doubt. Although part of The Balmoral Hotel the restaurant has created a reputation in its own right for fine dining - executive chef Jeff Bland whose culinary expertise is well known displays a quality of skills which have brought him recognition from many agencies and a number of awards. Jeff is equally at home with modern or traditional dishes - good combinations showing flair and imagination. High technical skills with some innovation, good texture and taste. There can be no doubt that diners' expectations are fully realised - also a fine wine list available for the connoisseur. Ambience perfect with fine furnishings and white linen - sound advice and service impeccable. **Michelin Star**. Restaurant Manager: Gary Quinn. (First visited, 2002). *AA* 🏵🏵🏵 🍴

Open: *Closed first 2 weeks January*		**Disabled:** *Access available*	**Covers:** *55*
Monday - Sunday: 6pm - 10.30pm		**Price Guide:** *3 course a la carte £75 (excluding wine)*	
No Rooms: *188*		*Chef's Tasting Menu £85 - £110.00*	
TV in Rooms: *Yes* **Room Tel.** *Yes*		*(add £55 for wine pairings)*	
Children: *Yes*		**Location:** *1 Princes Street*	

STAC POLLY RESTAURANT

29-33 Dublin Street, Edinburgh. EH3 6NL
Tel: 0131 556 2231
www.stacpolly.co.uk

Charismatic owner, Roger Coulthard, has been a permanent fixture in the Edinburgh culinary scene for as long as I can remember. The name Stac Polly comes from the famous Scottish mountain near Achiltibuie in the North West region of the country. Scottish fayre at its best with some European influences. Menus are carefully compiled to offer seasonal dishes which have been sourced with care, using good quality suppliers. Terrific wine cellar. Roger has refurbished the ground floor level and introduced a brasserie with the novelty of a gin and wine bar. The fine dining area remains downstairs. It takes a lot of stamina to maintain such a good reputation over so many years but Stac Polly has survived where others have failed. (First visited, 1989).

Open: *All year*		**Disabled:**	*Unsuitable*
No Rooms: *N/A*		**Covers:**	*40*
TV in Rooms: *N/A*		**Price Guide:**	*Lunch: £15.00-£18.00 (2 courses)*
Room Tel. *N/A*			*Dinner: £30.00-£40.00 (a la carte)*
Children: *Yes*		**Location:**	*Nr St Andrews Square. New Town - Central*

EAT ON THE GREEN

Udny Green, Ellon, Aberdeenshire. AB41 7RS
Tel: 01651 842337 Fax: 01651 843362
Email: enquiries@eatonthegreen.co.uk www.eatonthegreen.co.uk

Attractive rural location overlooking the village green at Udny not far from Ellon and Pitmedden Gardens (NTS). Charismatic 'kilted chef' Craig Wilson and his wife Lindsay have certainly created a food haven that is a must for the real 'foodie' - one not to be missed when visiting this part of Aberdeenshire. This restaurant has elicited praise from food critics and demanding food guides. I always look forward to my visits here – professional 'front of house' operation and a great dining experience in comfortable surroundings – clothed tables and relaxed ambience sets the tone. The secret here is the sourcing of quality ingredients and homegrown fruit and vegetables. Nothing complicated here (but some innovation) with clarity of flavour and consistent throughout all courses. Newly refurbished, comprising a stylish bar, champagne lounge, main restaurant and four elegant private dining rooms, Eat on the Green provides a venue appropriate for every occasion no matter how big or small. (Please see Food Foreword on page ..) Highly recommended. **AA** 🏵🏵 🍽

Open: *Closed Mon/Tues*		**Price Guide:** *Lunch: £23.95 - £26.95 (Weekdays)*	
Children: *Yes*		*Lunch: £29.95 - £34.95 (Sundays)*	
Disabled: *Yes*	**Covers:** *80*	*Sat. Eve. £59.00 (Canapes, rolls, 4 courses, coffee, petit four)*	
Location: *A920 from Ellon. B999 from*		*Tasting Menu £80 (£115 with matched wine)*	
Aberdeen. (Nr Pitmedden Gardens)		*Afternoon Tea £24 (£31.50 with glass champagne)*	

Derek Johnstone
Chef/Proprietor - Golf Inn
Gullane, East Lothian

STRAVAIGIN

28 Gibson Street, Hillhead, Glasgow. G12 8NX
Tel: 0141 334 2665   Fax: 0141 334 4099.
Email: bookings@stravaigin.com   www.stravaigin.com

Now a household name in Glasgow Stravaigin has taken on a 'new look' – the traditional Scottish roots are still apparent with the introduction of a more classical and contempory style. Difficult to describe the ambience here – certainly different and unusual. Bistro bordering on fine dining with some really wonderful combinations. Chilean stew of seafood and meats with Scottish mussels, lamb and rabbit. Aberdeen Angus sirloin topped with cajun styled prawns could be your choice. Catering for an ever evolving customer who require something different it has become more evident over the years that tastes and trends are changing. Stravaigin has introduced this innovative style of fusion which attracts its faithful followers. Sunday brunch a great experience. Good 'front of house' with staff who have been here for a few years and an extensive wine cellar add to the dining experience. Good value for money. 2 AA rosette award and Michelin Bib Gourmand 2012 and 2013. (First visited, 1990). *AA* ⊛⊛ 🍴

Open: *All year ex. Xmas, New Year & Sundays*		**Covers:**	*76*
No Rooms: *N/A*		**Price Guide:**	*Dinner from £25.00 - £30.00 (3 courses & a la carte)*
TV in Rooms: *N/A* **Room Tel.** *N/A*			*Lunch from £12.95 (2 courses)*
Children: *Yes*		**Location:**	*M8, junct 17 or A82 from city centre - Gt Western road, turn down park road, rt into Gibson St., 200 yds on right*
Disabled: *Unsuitable*			

THE GOLF INN

Main Street, Gullane, East Lothian. EH31 2AB
Tel: 01620 843259
Email: stay@golfinn.co.uk   www.golfinn.co.uk

Established in 1836, The Golf Inn is synonymous with the 'golfing burgh' of Gullane in this beautiful part of East Lothian – renowned for its many golf courses and seaside attractions. No doubt the 'heart of the community' it has recently been extensively refurbished - a massive task with impressive results. Could be described as a 'restaurant with rooms', there are 9 Deluxe Double ensuite bedrooms and two suites which can sleep 4. Absolute luxury with bespoke furnishings and superior ensuite amenities. Derek Johnstone (ex Head Chef at Greywalls) was the winner (2008) of the BBC's inaugural demanding Master Chef of the Year Award and his culinary talents are obvious whether you dine informally in the bar area or more formally in the main dining room. The motto here is 'the best guarantee of having a tasty product is to respect the season of every ingredient'. The ambience of a country inn has been retained – friendly, relaxed but very efficient. Function room available for that special occasion. Perfect location to avoid the 'hustle and bustle' of Edinburgh. 🍴

Open: *All year except Xmas Day*		**Price Guide:**	*Double £150.00 - £180.00*
No Rooms: *9 deluxe and 2 suites*			*Single £80.00 - £120.00*
TV in Rooms: *Yes* **Room Tel.** *Yes*			*Suite £250.00 - £400.00*
Children: *Yes* **Pets:** *No*			*Lunch & Dinner: from £25.95 (3 courses)*
Disabled: *Dining only*		**Location:**	*Main Street, Gullane*

www.champagne-billecart.fr

ROCPOOL RESTAURANT

1 Ness Walk, Inverness. IV3 5NE
Tel: 01463 717274
Email: info@rocpoolrestaurant.com   www.rocpoolrestaurant.com

Highly rated restaurant on the banks of the River Ness – ideal corner location on the main 'drag' through the City. Chef/proprietor, Steven Devlin, known to me for many years and indeed before he opened his own venture in 2002. Despite his reluctance for publicity he enjoys a tremendous amount of loyal support and the proof as they say is 'in the eating'. A culinary master and technician, Steven revels in his passion for food whether classical or modern in concept. He introduces innovation with some imaginative combinations which work perfectly. Seasonal produce from quality suppliers and a dedicated kitchen staff and you have the perfect formula. Dining area is contemporary/modern 'surrounded' by glass windows – ambience of an artistic nature. Menus offer good choice including an early evening meal (except Saturday) at £16.95 for 2 courses. Ideal before you head off to the Eden Court Theatre just 'up the road'. Certainly one for 'the foodies'. Highly recommended. *AA* ❀❀

Open: *All year except Sudays*	**Covers:**	*36*
No Rooms: *N/A*	**Price Guide:**	*Lunch £15.95 (2 course)*
TV in Rooms: *N/A* **Room Tel.** *N/A*		*Early evening meal £17.95 (2 course)*
Children: *Yes*		*Dinner £25.00 - £37.50 (a la carte)*
Disabled: *Yes*	**Location:**	*Corner Ardross/Ness Walk. Centre of Inverness*

THE GROUSE AND CLARET RESTAURANT

Heatheryford, Kinross. KY13 ONQ
Tel: 01577 864212
Email: grouseandclaret@lineone.net   www.grouseandclaret.com

The Grouse and Claret Country Centre combines restaurant, accommodation, art gallery and fishery. It is very conveniently situated between Edinburgh and Perth, just off the M90 at Junction 6, set in a rural setting with 25 acres gardens, meadow and lochans. Your hosts, chef/proprietor David Futong and his wife Vicki, have earned an enviable reputation over 24 years for quality cuisine in an ideal setting. Menus are changed seasonally and cater for all tastes, using predominantly locally sourced produce with great emphasis on delicious home made food, beautifully presented and with some Oriental dishes. The Gallery is ideal for small country weddings and family celebrations. Comfortable detached bedrooms - some overlooking the trout ponds - make this the ideal base in the country only a short 30 minutes drive from the city of Edinburgh. Ample car parking. (First visited, 1998).

Open: *All year ex. 1 wk. Jan; 10 days Nov.*	**Disabled:** *Yes*	**Covers:**	*60*
Closed Sun. night & all day Mon.	**Price Guide:** *B&B price per room: From £50.00 per person*		
No Rooms: *3 En Suite 3*	*Lunch £10.50 - £20.00*		
TV in Rooms: *Yes* **Room Tel.** *No*	*Dinner £20.00 - £35.00 (à la carte)*		
	Location: *Leave M90 Junction 6 then 500 yds -*		
Children: *Yes*	*take the private road opposite service station*		

Darren Miranda
Head Chef - Horseshoe Restaurant
Eddleston, nr. Peebles

LIVINGSTON'S RESTAURANT

52 High Street, Linlithgow, West Lothian. EH49 7AE
Tel: 01506 846565
Email: contact@livingstons-restaurant.co.uk   www.livingstons-restaurant.co.uk

This is what you call a real hidden gem of a restaurant. A 'cottage' themed restaurant set in attractive gardens it is located through a vennel off the main street. The new extension fits in perfectly with the original rustic type dining room. A family business in the true sense of the word, this is a great success story which has been built up by the Livingston family over a number of years. Changing direction slightly, a semi-bistro policy has been adopted here, but there is no compromise with the quality of the food and beverage operation. All dishes are consistent with vibrant flavours and this is consistent with all courses. A sign of the times - we have to adapt to the demands of our customers! Great ambience and certainly value for money. Wine cellar of note. A thriving restaurant with a high percentage of repeat business. Your hosts: Ronald, Christine and Derek Livingston. (First visited, 1999). *AA* 🏵🏵

Open: *Closed Sun/Mon & 1st 2 weeks Jan and 1 week June & Oct*		**Disabled:** *Yes*	
No Rooms: *N/A*		**Covers:** *50*	
TV in Rooms: *N/A* **Room Tel.** *N/A*		**Price Guide:** *Lunch £12.50 - £20.00*	
Children: *Over 8 (evening)*			*Dinner £15.00 - £40.00*
		Location:	*Eastern end of High Street opp. Post Office.*

THE HORSESHOE RESTAURANT WITH ROOMS

Eddleston Village, Edinburgh Road, Nr. Peebles. EH45 8QP
Tel: 01721 730225
Email: reservations@horseshoeinn.co.uk   www.horseshoeinn.co.uk

Forging ahead and eliciting praise from a number of press sources this is one for the real food connoisseur. Talents of head chef Darren Miranda and his kitchen brigade are evident - greater technical skills with great consistency and judgement (some innovation) and a clear ambition to achieve high standards. Emphasis here on local fresh seasonal produce - listed quality suppliers. Sophisticated wine cellar. Several visits this year - meals perfectly executed and expectations met. Excellent value for money too – varies from £20 for a 2 course lunch to £50 for an a la carte dinner or £60 for the tasting menu option. Service is warm, genuine and personal. There are 8 delightful bedrooms at the rear of the premises with ample car parking. Disabled designated with ramp. An ideal retreat on the periphery of Edinburgh. Your host: General Manager: Mark Slaney. 🐷

Open: *All year*		**Price Guide:** *Rooms Double £130.00*	
No Rooms: 8		*Lunch £20.00 (2 courses); £25.00 (3 courses)*	
TV in Rooms: *Yes*		*Dinner £50.00 (a la carte); £60.00 (tasting menu)*	
Room Tel. *Yes*	**Disabled:** *Dining only*	**Location:** *20 mls south of Edinburgh on A703,*	
Children: *Yes*	**Covers:** 36	*5 mls north of Peebles*	

63 TAY STREET

63 Tay Street, Perth. PH2 8NN

Tel: 01738 441451

Email: info@63taystreet.com   www.63taystreet.com

Great location just on the periphery of the city overlooking the River Tay. There has been a recent 'makeover' of the interior which generates a great ambience. Over the years Master Chef of Great Britain Graeme Pallister has won numerous awards – his talents and dedication are beyond reproach and there is always this driving ambition to achieve high standards. Careful sourcing (suppliers listed on menu), careful prep and always signs of innovation prevail. Garden Pea Soup with East Neuk Mackerel, curry, Scrabster hake fillet and an excellent lemon and poppy seed cake could be your choice. Varied menus for lunch and pre-theatre, dinner and a 5 course tasting menu are available. Manager Lukas on hand to advise on a great wine cellar. Definite food destination for the real 'foodie' not to be missed. Service was faultless. (Also see entry for The Parklands Hotel within this publication.) Highly commended. *AA*🏵 🏵 ☕

Open: *All year ex. Sun & Mon*		**Covers:**	*32*
No Rooms: *N/A*		**Price Guide:**	*Tasting Menu £45.00*
TV in Rooms: *N/A* **Room Tel.** *N/A*			*Lunch & Pre-theatre £13.00 - £22.00*
Children: *Yes, but no separate menu*			*Dinner £34.00 - £39.00*
Disabled: *Yes*		**Location:**	*63 Tay Street, beside the river*

ALBERT & MICHEL ROUX Jnr AT INVERLOCHY CASTLE

Torlundy, Fort William. PH33 6SN

Tel: 01397 702177

Email: info@inverlochy.co.uk www.inverlochycastlehotel.com www.icmi.co.uk

A family enterprise by the renowned Roux family. Albert Roux has been associated with the Inverlochy Management Group for some years and is now joined by the well known TV personality and family member Michel Roux at Inverlochy Castle. Andrew Turnbull has been appointed head chef (see hotel entry for Inverlochy Castle) but the Roux influence is prevalent. Whether classical or traditional this is a gastronomic delight with innovation and evolving concepts. Great technical skills and dedication to produce a wonderful dining experience. Albert Roux OBE, KFO, who is head of the famous cooking dynasty, was behind such establishments as Le Gavroche which was the first ever restaurant in the UK to be awarded 3 Michelin Stars. This restaurant within Inverlochy Castle aspires to be one of the premier food destinations in the country and I have never been disappointed. Highly recommended. (First visited 1993). *AA*🏵 🏵 🏵 ★★★★★ ☕

Open: *All year*		**Conference Facilities:** *Small - Director level*		
No Rooms: *18 En Suite 18*		**Price Guide:** *Dinner £67.00*		
TV in Rooms: *Yes* **Pets:** *Yes*		*(See hotel entry for room prices)*		
Children: *Yes* **Disabled:** *Yes*	**Location:**	*Village of Torlundy 3 mls north of*		
Swimming Pool/Health Club: *No*		*Ft William on A82*		

WINDLESTRAW

Walkerburn, Peeblesshire.EH43 6AA
Tel: 01896 870636
Email: stay@windlestraw.co.uk www.windlestraw.co.uk

Just on the periphery of Walkerburn in the borders this is a very attractive country house situated in magnificent garden policies. The home of John and Sylvia Matthews, my visit for dinner was prompted by others who had been before me. As I discovered this could well be a 'restaurant with rooms' – there are 6 luxurious bedrooms which would grace any premier country house hotel. Certainly a gastronomic triumph and my expectations were fully met. Wonderful canapes sets the theme – 6 course menu with the hake and venison dishes perfectly cooked. Complete dedication here – technical skills evident in every dish. Consistent throughout and perfectly executed. Daily changing menus mandatory here and aspirations to achieve high standards. Great ambience. Make sure this is included in your itinery when you visit this part of the country. Highly recommended.

Open: *All year (ex. Dec-Feb)*	**Disabled:** *Not suitable*	**Covers:** *20*
No Rooms: *6 ensuite 6*	**Price Guide:** *Double £175.00 - £275.00 Dinner £50.00*	
TV in Rooms: *Yes*	**Location:** *Edinburgh/Peebles then A72 to Walkerburn*	
Room Tel. *Yes*	*(8 miles) (Just be careful at the entrance from*	
Children: *Yes*	*the main road.)*	

ASSOCIATE RESTAURANT - N. IRELAND   *BELFAST*

DEANES

36-40 Howard Street, Belfast. BT1 6PF
Tel: 02890 331134
Email: info@michaeldeane.co.uk www.michaeldeane.co.uk

Eipic is the most recent and most sophisticated of the restaurants in Michael Deane's portfolio. Still located in Howard Street it has recently been completely refurbished. A great success story from the time I met him in Scotland in 1988. His exhuberant style - both of showmanship and of uncompromisingly perfectionist cooking has elicited praise from the sternest of food critics and the most demanding food guides. Since 2010 Michael has changed his menus to reflect a more 'down to earth' approach and can now be classified as more Irish traditional with a hint of French influence. Specialist suppliers and great prep work here - food produced to a very high standard. From his beginnings at Claridges Michael has been on a pilgrimage - always propelled by his pure passion for food and its possibilities. 3 AA food rosettes since 1997. (**Michelin Star** awarded for 2016). Keep this one in mind and follow this entry whenever in Belfast. *AA*❀❀❀

Open: *Closed Sun.-Tues.*	**Disabled:** *Brasserie only*
No Rooms: *N/A*	**Covers:** *35*
TV in Rooms: *N/A* **Room Tel.** *N/A*	**Price Guide:** *Dinner £40.00 - £60.00*
Children: *Welcome*	*Lunch: Brasserie - from £30.00*

The Wine Column

The Duty Faced by a Sommelier

I have recently returned from two weeks of checking out some Michelin restaurants in Spain. Whilst the sommeliers there face the same duty as sommeliers here – to create interesting wines lists that showcase the best wines that are being made today, in Spain there is evidently not another duty that they face, unlike here. That is the duty imposed by HMRC.

The cost in duty and vat means, comparing like with like between Spain and here is almost unfair. Add to that shipping costs and more significantly wine merchants' margins here and buying wine in a restaurant here is pricey, whilst buying in Spain is a joy.

A decent bottle of Albarino in a smart restaurant in Spain is roughly 50% less expensive than buying the same wine in a restaurant here. In one restaurant, that I went to in Leon, a three course set lunch at 17 Euros not only included a main course of sea bass or sirloin of young bull but a 250ml carafe of wine was thrown in as well. In the heart of Madrid, the two Michelin Star Club El Allard offers a stunning wine list but the prices are refreshingly sane. At a tapas bar in the same city, Celso y Manolo, there is a selection of unusual organic and natural wines by the glass, the priciest of which was only 3.25 euros. A Demontro Cantorres Ampurdia natural Garnacha, cloudy and the colour of crushed raspberries, tasted fabulous and a Neno di Vina Somoza 2014 from Valdeorras was the best Godello that I have tasted.

Natural wines, organic wines and bio-dynamic wines certainly seem to be more and more in demand these days. They were very much in evidence in Spain and when I was in Copenhagen, earlier in the year, they were dominating the Michelin restaurants wine lists and especially the wines by the glass offerings.

At Amass, in Copenhagen, I drank a natural Chenin Blanc from Escoda Sanahuja from Conca de Barbera, (425DKK) made by Jon Ramon, which was excellent. The colour of old cider, the wine was dry, full bodied, slightly petillant at the start and had a mouth filling apple flavour with a strong, long finish. A biodynamic red from Jura, Le Jaja du Bon from Jean Francois Greneat was also good. Indigo no.1 Teauben, Liebe and Zeit, Blauen Wildbacher from Stiererland, Austria was interesting but its sweet perfume was too intrusive for me. The wine list, focused heavily on natural and biodynamic wines, made for fascinating reading. The Head Chef, Matt Orlando, was previously Sous Chef at Noma and Amass, not surprisingly, now has a serious following.

More exciting for me though was Kjobenhavn Bistro. Rasmus Lund Jonasson. the Head Chef here, used to work in the Michelin starred AOC. The bistro is small and the tiny, open plan kitchen is just about big enough for a chef to swing a herring and there were three guys squeezed into it; two chefs and a washer-up, by my reckoning. Not only was the food bang on the nail here but the wine list was too. We drank a bottle of Elena Wach 'Ludwig' Pinot Noir from the Alto Adige (500DKK). When I asked the waitress, half way through our tasting menu dinner, to choose a second bottle of something similar but different, a Napa Pinot arrived in seconds and, a nice touch, the waitress smelt and then tasted the wine, so there was no delay before our (fresh) glasses were before us and filled.

So, coming back to the duty faced by a sommelier; maybe making sure all the front of house team have an appreciation of the wines offered by the glass, might be one such duty? Obviously, not every member of the waiting team can know the wine list inside out, but it is so refreshing to be somewhere where the staff know more than you might expect, and therein, be able to respond quickly and efficiently to a customers' needs. It is common practice now in decent restaurants for the staff to have a food briefing prior to each service; surely an extra five minutes spent on wine appreciation wouldn't go amiss?

Mark Slaney is a fine dining consultant, wine writer and a member of the Society of Authors. His book on wine, 'Tasting Notes' is published in paperback.

www.markslaneyassociates.com

THE WINE COLUMN

Dark Chocolate Torte with Aberdeenshire Barra Berries and Homegrown Flowers

Gingernut Biscuits:

230g plain flour
2tsp baking powder
2tsp mixed spice
1tsp cinnamon
115g Caster Sugar

4tbls syrup
115g soft butter
2tsp ginger
2tsp bicarbonate of soda
0.5tsp salt

Combine all ingredients and press into a lined tray. Put into a pre-heated oven at 180deg for 15-20mins until golden.

Base:

800g ginger nut biscuits
300g Scottish butter, melted
pinch of sea salt
100g cocoa powder

Blitz biscuits to a fine crumb, add melted butter, salt and cocoa powder; mix well and press into a 30x60cm tray.

Chocolate Filling:

750g dark chocolate
350g Scottish butter
800ml Scottish cream

5g sea salt
90g local honey

Put chocolate, butter and honey in a bowl. Bring honey and cream to the boil then pour over the chocolate, butter and honey. Mix well; pour onto base and leave to chill.

Honeycomb:

300g caster sugar
25g glucose
90ml local honey

10ml water
25g bicarbonate of soda

Put all ingredients in to a pan apart from bicarbonate of soda. Bring to a caramel then whisk in bicarbonate of soda thoroughly. Pour in to a tray and leave to set.

Strawberry & Raspberry Puree:

500g raspberry puree from local berries
500g strawberry puree from local berries
12g Agar Agar

Add both purees to a pan, bring to a boil. Add agar agar, simmer for two minutes and then pour into a tray. Leave to set and cool. Blitz into a smooth puree.

Chef/Proprietor: Craig Wilson
Eat on the Green, Udny Green, Ellon, Aberdeenshire
(also see entry page 73)

Turbot, Chorizo Stew and Curried Courgette Foam

(Serves 4)

Ingredients:

4 x 5oz fillets of turbot
(Most fishmongers will fillet this down for you as it has to be cut
into 5 to 7oz portions. If you feel this is on the pricey side
you could use hake or cod).

For the stew:

500g Chorizo Rosario (chopped)
400g tin cannellini Beans
250g chopped peppers
250g red onions
250g courgettes
1kg vine tomatoes (blanched and peeled)
100g chopped coriander

For the Foam:

400g peeled courgettes (keep green peel for later)
500mls fish stock (can buy from shop ready made)
20g Madras curry powder

Method:

For the chorizo stew you need to cut all the ingredients down to the same size. Start by putting 50mls of good rapeseed oil in a thick-bottomed pan, add the red onions and chorizo and cook down on a high heat string all the time. After around 10 minutes, add the rest of the ingredients to the pan. Add 300mls of water and let it reduce. Then take the tomatoes and blanch in boiling water for 30 seconds. Remove them and add straight to iced water. (The skins will come off easily after that.) Add the tomatoes to the stew and turn down to a very low heat and cook out for 50 minutes, stirring every ten minutes.

For the courgette, add 25mls of oil to pan, put the peeled and chopped courgettes in pan, add curry powder and cook out on a high heat for 10 minutes until the

spices have infused well. Add the fish stock and turn down - the stock needs to reduce by half. Cook for 30 minutes and blitz down until smooth. Just before you remove from the food processor, add the green peeling back in and blitz down until it turns green. Pass through a strainer and leave aside to cool.

For the fish, lightly dust in flour and pan roast with some thyme, garlic and lots of butter. Finish under the grill. Place the fish on a cloth to drain before plating.

To Serve:

Add the stew to the bottom of a bowl and place the fish on top. Take the courgette and, with a hand Blitzer, foam up. Add the foam to the plate and dress with some edible flowers.

Head Chef: Grant MacNicol
Fonab Castle & Spa, Pitlochry, Perthshire
(also see entry page 47)

Hake with Squat Lobster,
Sharpes Express Potato and Rice Cracker

Whilst hake is fairly readily available and not expensive, squat lobsters are harder to get hold of and their season is limited. They are, though, utterly delicious and this dish, whilst it is a bit time consuming to get prepared, is a great way to enjoy them. If you don't have a vac-pack machine, a water bath and a deep fat fryer, don't panic, see the notes at the end of the recipe.

Ingredients:

200g hake lightly cured for 10 minutes	140g ginger
200g Sharpes Express potatoes peeled	4 lemon grass
1kg squat lobsters	2 heads of garlic
3kg plum tomatoes	1 lime
100g long grain rice	200g butter
1 litre water	

Preparation:

Blend the tomatoes, hang them in a muslin bag, collect the juice that oozes out overnight into a dish. The next day, put the juice into pan and reduce it slowly until it's two thirds the quantity that it was originally. The pulp in the muslin you can use for something else – maybe on some homemade pizza. Peel the squat lobsters, removing the long, thin black string that shouldn't be eaten. Blend the shells with 1 litre of water, 50g ginger, 2 lemon grass, 3 cloves garlic and in a sauce pan, bring to a simmer then simmer for 30 minutes, skim it regularly then pass the mixture through muslin. Peel and de-seed three further plum tomatoes and compress them in a vac pack machine with a teaspoon of reduced tomato water.

Cook rice with 200ml of reserved squat lobster stock and 200ml of water. Once the rice is almost dry blend with 40 grams of raw squat lobsters and spread evenly over parchment paper and dehydrate for 24 – 48 hours until completely dry. Line the bottom of a steamer pan with tin foil, cover with oak smoking chips and heat on medium to high. Put peeled potatoes into steamer. Once the chips begin to smoke put potatoes over and cover. Smoke for 10 to 15 minutes until potatoes have turned a rich yellow colour, remove potatoes and vacuum seal on full with some butter. Cook sous vide at 87deg C. for 1 hour. Once cooked, cool. Dice 2/3 potatoes into an even size, then warm gently in a little butter. In a pan mix 2 tablespoons of reduced squat's stock with 1 tablespoon of reduced tomato water, then warm but do not boil. In a steamer pan add garlic, lemon grass, ginger, lime + 300ml water, bring to the boil, steam hake for 5-8 minutes. Dice compressed tomato and add to warm potato.

To Serve:

Place the diced tomato and warm potatoes in a dish/plate for each person and add the steamed fish on top. Carefully pour around the hake the tomato and lobster juice. Finally place the cracker on top and garnish with micro leaves.

Kitchen Equipment:

Instead of a vacuum machine use a zip lock bag with as much of the air removed as possible. Instead of a water bath use a pan of water. Use a thermometer to check the temperature which should be above 85deg but below boiling. Instead of a deep fat fryer a high sided pan a quarter full of oil will suffice. Using a thermometer bring the oil to 170deg and make sure it doesn't rise to above 180deg.

Head Chef: Darren Miranda
Horseshoe Restaurant, Peebles
(also see entry page 79)

Scotch Pork Cheek, Black Pudding 'Scotch Egg', Soft Polenta, Braised Lettuce & Bacon, Peas

For the Cheeks:

4 x large Scotch pigs' cheeks
1 carrot
1 stick celery
2 star anise
2 shallots
2 sprigs rosemary

2 sprigs thyme
2 cloves garlic
1 ltr rich chicken or veal stock
2tsp redcurrant jelly
1 glass red wine
a few whole peppercorns

Season and seal the pork cheeks in a hot pan and remove to a pressure cooker. In the same pan sweat the vegetables (peeled and roughly chopped), garlic and herbs and add to the pressure cooker. Add the stock, wine, peppercorns, star anise and jelly. Seal the presure cooker and cook at full pressure for 30 mins. Remove cheeks and set aside. Strain and reduce stock to a glaze. Add cheeks back to the reduced stock and baste until warmed through.

For the Black Pudding Scotch Egg:

4 Scottish quails eggs, soft boiled and peeled
Stornaway black pudding
Flour, eggwash, panko breadcrumbs and seeds to pané

Soften black pudding in a mixer or by working with your hands. Wrap each quails egg in black pudding and roll into a ball. Pane with the panko crumbs mixed with some seeds. (I use onion and sesame seeds.) Deep fry until golden

For the Soft Polenta:

100ml chicken stock
100ml cream
1 clove garlic, crushed
1 tsp chopped chives

100g Polenta cornmeal
50g grated Isle of Mull Cheddar
or Parmesan
(but I prefer to use Scottish cheese!)

Bring the stock, cream and garlic to the boil. Reduce heat to a simmer and 'rain' in polenta, stirring all the time. Cook until thick and the polenta is no longer 'grainy'. Season and add the cheese and herbs. Serve immediately.

For the Lettuce & Bacon:

1 head of baby gem lettuce
75g smoked streaky bacon, diced
1 small shallot, finely chopped
1/2 clove garlc, crushed

A handful of fresh peas, blanched
50ml chicken stock
50ml cream

In a pan, caramelise the bacon. Reduce the heat and add the shallots and garlic, sweat until transluscent. Add the cream and stock and bring to the boil, reducing by half. Add the leaves of lettuce and the peas and allow to wilt and warm through. Season and serve immediately.

For the Pea Sauce:

200ml chicken stock	Seeds from 1/4 vanilla pod
50g butter	Salt and pepper
400g green peas	Lemon juice

Boil stock, butter and vanilla. Add peas and bring back to the boil. Immediately puree and strain. Season with salt, pepper and a dash of lemon juice. Serve warm.

Head Chef/Proprietor: David Littlewood
The Kildrummy Inn, Alford
(also see entry page 63)

Chocolate Pudding (orange) with Vanilla Ice Cream
(Serves 24)

Ganache:

1 ltr water
300g sugar
100g cocoapowder
700g dark orange couverture

Bring water and sugar to boil. whisk onto cocoa powder mix in chocolate until smooth. Pour into rings lined with cling film and freeze.

Sponge:

550g dark orange chocolate
250g butter
200g ground almonds
200g cornflower
15 egg yolks
15 egg whites
400g sugar

Melt chocolate together with butter, mix in ground almonds and cornflower, then mix in yolks. Whisk whites with sugar to firm reaks. Fold into chocolate batter. Pipe into rings lined double with paper. Place frozen ganache in centre, top with more sponge to seal, store in freezer.

Vanilla Ice Cream:

1 ltr milk
500ml dbl cream
8 vanilla pods
6 coffee beans, crushed
12 egg yolks
340g caster sugar

Scrape vanilla pods, place pods in saucepan with milk and crushed coffee and bring to boil. Remove from heat, cover and infuse for 10min. Whisk yolks with sugar and vanilla seeds till light and pale. Re-boil milk and mix into yolks. Return to heat to thicken. Add cream, cool, strain through chinois, churn and freeze.

Crème Anglaise (extra thick):

275ml milk
275ml dbl cream
115g caster sugar
1 vanilla pod, scraped
10 yolks

Bring milk, cream, sugar and vanilla to boil. Whisk together yolks and remaining sugar and pour on boiling milk. Mix well and return to heat to thicken. Add cream andchinois into bowl over ice bain marie, prevent curdling.

Chef: Andrew Fairlie
The Gleneagles Hotel, Auchterarder, Perthshire
(also see entry page 65)

STEVENSONS

SCOTLAND'S
GOOD HOTEL AND FOOD BOOK
2017

Order Form: **Alan Stevenson Publications
Fala, 20 West Cairn Crescent, Penicuik,
Midlothian EH26 0AR
Tel: 01968 678015
E-mail: alan@stevensons-scotland.com**

Date: .... Please mail .... Copies of

Stevensons, Scotland's Good Hotel and Food Book, 2017. (22nd Edition)

Your Name: ....

Address: ....

.... Postcode: ....

Retail Price
(All prices include postage and packaging)

United Kingdom	**£12.00**
Euro Zone	**€24.00**
Outside Europe	**£20.00**
USA only	**$28.00**
Canada only	**$30.00**

Alternatively purchase online at www.stevensons-scotland.com
Multiple orders: price on application
Orders outwith the UK consigned by airmail
Payment in pounds sterling payable to Alan Stevenson Publications

No. of Copies: ...... at £/$/€.............. each. Total £/$/€ ....

I enclose a Cheque/Bank Draft   Total £/$/€ ....

Hotels continued

Restaurants listed alphabetically by name

Hotels listed alphabetically by name

See contents page 4 for list of Trade Sponsors.